"Of all the reputed relics of Christ's crucifixion —vials of his blood, nails from his hands and forests of splinters from 'the true cross'— none holds more fascination for believers and skeptics alike than the mysterious 'Holy Shroud of Turin' . . . an amazingly detailed picture of a bearded man who had been beaten about the body, crowned with thorns and pierced with nails through the wrists and feet. In short, the Shroud itself appears to be a negative of a body."     —*Newsweek*

"In all my years of experience with pictorial productions I have yet to see anything that approximates the image on the Shroud. That so incomparable a portrait of Christ, with no visible trace of paint, should be found *in reverse* on an ancient cloth, is an enigma to which we art experts do not have a solution."
—C. D. Viale, art expert

"The Shroud is explicable if it once enwrapped a human body to which something extraordinary happened. It is not explicable otherwise."     —Geoffrey Ashe, British scholar

**THE FIFTH GOSPEL**
is an original Pocket Book edition.

# THE
# FIFTH GOSPEL

*The Miracle of the Holy Shroud*

by Thomas Humber

PUBLISHED BY POCKET BOOKS NEW YORK

To Lorrel and Christopher
who endure

# Acknowledgments

I am neither a scholar nor a scientist, and this book is largely the product of secondary research, an attempt to present clearly in one accessible volume the complex story of the Shroud of Turin. In this task, I have been amply aided by those who have gone before, largely unheralded in the eyes of the general public. I am particularly indebted to the research and writings of Mr. John Walsh, Dr. Paul Joseph Vignon, Dr. Pierre Barbet, Professor Werner Bulst, Dr. David Willis, the Reverend Edward A. Wuenschel and the Reverend Maurus Green.

Words can never sufficiently express my appreciation to the Reverend Peter M. Rinaldi, who gave me his time, his wisdom and his aid at every step, often at sacrifice to his own important work. The fact that the Shroud of Turin is known at all in this country is largely due to the efforts of Father Rinaldi and the Reverend Adam J. Otterbein, and for that we should all be thankful to them.

If this book has any originality or importance at all, the efforts of Peter A. Tscherning deserve much of the credit. His ability as a linguist, his tenacity as a researcher and his brilliance as a scholar made a frighteningly complicated task manageable.

The people mentioned above have either knowingly or unknowingly contributed to my ability to write this book. They are not, however, in any way responsible for any misinterpretations or factual inaccuracies into which I might have blundered, nor should my acknowledgment of their contributions be taken to mean that any of them subscribe to either my presentation or conclusions.

# Contents

*A 16-page photographic insert appears
between pages 88 and 89.*

# Introduction

For over six hundred years, an international storm of controversy has raged over an ancient strip of linen known simply as the Shroud of Turin. Thousands of books and articles have been written about it. Millions of people have made the pilgrimage to see it on those rare occasions when it has been exposed to public view.

The Shroud, photographs of it and its fragmentary history have been studied by scholars, historians, scientists of many disciplines, artists, textile experts and self-proclaimed authorities. It has been attacked by religious men of great faith, and it has been defended with equal, if not greater, vehemence by confirmed agnostics.

Regardless of the attention it has received, the Shroud remains virtually unknown in the English-speaking world, and its essential mysteries remain unsolved to this date. Is this remarkable cloth—with its clearly visible images of a man who was scourged mercilessly, humiliated by a crown of thorns, forced to bear his own cross, and finally crucified and gashed in his side to assure his death, all in accord with the Gospel descriptions of the Holy Passion—is this yellowed cloth the true burial shroud of Jesus

11

Christ? Or is it the most ingenious and perplexing forgery the world has ever seen?

If it is authentic, the Holy Shroud is unquestionably the greatest religious relic known to Christianity and one of the most fascinating antiquities known to mankind. If it is authentic, the Shroud can rightfully take its place as "The Fifth Gospel," for what it reveals of Jesus and his suffering far exceeds the scant Gospel words of the evangelists. If it is authentic, and if no completely satisfactory natural explanation can account for its unusual physical properties, then the Shroud is indeed the most miraculous of Holy Miracles—an enduring, self-made portrait of the man who would be called Savior by millions of Christians throughout the world.

But what if the Shroud is a forgery, whether perpetrated for good or evil? Do we merely write it off as a clever hoax and forget it? I think not, for if the Shroud is a fake, then whoever fabricated it, by whatever unknown methods, had command of knowledge and abilities quite incredible for his time. Specifically, he must have known the precise methods of crucifixion of the period; he must have possessed the medical knowledge of a contemporary master surgeon; he must have utilized an art process unknown to any great master, never duplicated before or since; he must have been able to foresee and approximate principles of photography not otherwise discovered for centuries.

All of this had to have been done prior to 1356, for since that date the Shroud has a clearly documented and uninterrupted history. Impossible? Perhaps, but so, by some lights, are the statues of Easter Island, the Piri Reis maps and the astronomical calculations of Stonehenge. Even now, with all the scientific knowledge and technical skills at our command, the Shroud cannot be satisfactorily duplicated.

For many people, it may well be easier to accept the authenticity of the Shroud rather than face the almost insoluble mysteries it would present were it a fake. Two thousand years of Christian tradition is strong medicine, and even the most hardened skeptics have not been able to deny the historicity of Jesus or his crucifixion. What then, believers will ask, is so difficult about accepting the existence of a visible record of Jesus' last hours?

There are others who will be like Thomas, the doubting disciple. They will want to believe, but they must be shown; they must have tangible proof. To still others, the Shroud will not be a religious question at all, but a problem for science and archaeology, a challenge to the ability of contemporary man to gradually erase, one by one, the mysteries of the past so that he may better understand his future.

Regardless of prior orientation, the story of the Shroud is a fascinating one to Christian, agnostic, and atheist alike. But why, then, if the Shroud is so important, if the controversy over it has been so great, has it remained so obscure? Why have most people never heard of it, and if so, only vaguely? Why are the details of this centuries-old puzzle just now beginning to achieve the public prominence and study they deserve? Although they cannot easily be justified, there are ample reasons.

Primary among these is the fact that, prior to November 1973, the Shroud had been on public display only twice in this century—in 1931 and in 1933—and then only for a few days' duration. At

all other times it has been kept hidden away—
wrapped around a wooden pole, ensconced in a
long, silver reliquary—in a vault of the Royal Chapel
behind the chancel of the Cathedral of Turin, Italy.

Although actually owned by Humbert II of Savoy, the exiled king of Italy, the Shroud has for
centuries been under the care and supervision of the
Archdiocese of Turin. And until very recently the
hierarchy of the church had been strangely indis-
posed toward allowing sophisticated scientific investigation or any extended public display of the
Shroud. The reasons for their reluctance can only be
a matter of conjecture, since their intransigence has
been equaled only by their silence. Suffice it to say,
however, that their greatest sin has been one of
benign neglect, for no one who is knowledgeable
seriously believes in any conspiracy of suppression,
as has been charged from some quarters.

Contributing to the Shroud's obscurity is the fact
that in the early years of this century, several scath-
ing attacks on its authenticity by reputable scholars
in prestigious publications were potent enough to
severely stifle public interest. That these scholars
based their dismissals of the Shroud as a fraud solely
on several historical documents of dubious validity,
completely ignoring the more legitimate results of
scientific inquiry, did little to alleviate the damage.

The final reason for our lack of knowledge concerns the general inaccessibility of information about
the Shroud. Although books and articles on the subject number in the thousands, few have been popularly written and published, and only a handful have
appeared in English. Some of them, of course, have
been the works of crackpots and charlatans, to be
immediately dismissed; others the efforts of men

who found only what they sought, and who sought to make their genius more compelling than their evidence.

There are several seminal works that reveal prodigious research and tireless years of devotion to the subject. I am deeply indebted to the authors of these, for without their pioneering efforts, the Shroud would probably not have achieved the recognition it has, and without their descriptions of their findings this book would have been impossible. But by and large, these books and articles were neither written for, nor have they reached, the massive general audience that the Shroud demands.

*The Fifth Gospel* is an attempt to fill that void, to present a comprehensive yet lucid chronicle and appraisal of the Shroud to the widest possible audience. It is not an easy task, for to deal with the Shroud is to be catapulted into the complex worlds of archaeology, linguistics, exegesis, science, medicine, photography and history—all at the same time. The author can claim no particular authority in any of these fields; he is but a reporter who has sought first to understand the facts himself, and then to present them simply and fairly, without distortion. This, then, is a book for laymen by a layman.

It is purposefully not a book for scholars or critics; to discuss every critical or historical issue related to the Shroud would be to sacrifice clarity and readability, to produce a book so ponderous and so loaded with obscure references and petty detail that its goal would have been lost at the outset.

On November 23, 1973, the Shroud of Turin was placed on limited exhibition, via television, throughout parts of Europe and South America. The ceremony that was held preceded the turning over of the Shroud to an international commission of scientists who would attempt to determine, for once and for all, either the authenticity or illegitimacy of the Shroud. The results of their tests, however, will probably not be announced for at least a year, or more likely, several years. Until that time, it is hoped that this book will be a substantial contribution to the present state of knowledge of the Shroud of Turin.

T.H.
July 1974

# THE
# FIFTH GOSPEL

# I

## The "Photograph" of Jesus

The elaborate ceremony of displaying the Shroud had taken almost two hours. Mass had been said. One by one, the three locks securing its resting place had been opened. The seals on its outer box had been broken, the relic carefully extracted from its silver casket, unrolled and attached to its backing board and placed in its ornate frame. Now, the audience—royalty, church hierarchy, foreign dignitaries and privileged laymen—stared with rapt attention at the ancient cloth which hung above the marble altar in the magnificently appointed Cathedral of Saint John the Baptist in Turin, Italy.

Archbishop Agostino Richelmy slowly took his place in the pulpit. With his arms reverently raised to the enshrined cloth, he began to speak: "Behold above the altar the eternal monument to the sufferings of God crucified . . . come to look upon it, ye who adore the sublime beauty of Christianity; see how the ancient prophecy is fulfilled before our gaze. Immense is our good fortune that we have here this Holy Shroud . . . centuries have passed, the face of the earth has changed, yet the honors rendered to this sacred sheet have never ceased. . . . It is, of course, stained with blood . . . it describes His torment . . . it reveals His wounds. Come and gaze;

kneel down and pray; let tears stream unchecked from your eyes. Peter and John found this sacred sheet folded carefully inside the empty tomb. . . . I declare that in Thee, Most Sacred Shroud, the greatest of treasures was enclosed . . . for Thou didst enfold the divine Author of our Redemption."

It was May 25, 1898, and cities all over Italy were celebrating the fiftieth anniversary of the constitution of Sardinia, on which the laws of Italy were based. But no other city possessed so great an attraction as the Shroud of Turin, and during the eight days it would remain on public exposition, close to a million people would pass beneath it to offer their veneration. Although Archbishop Richelmy had seen it for the first time when it had been removed from its storage place that morning, his sermon left no room for doubt. He believed completely in the authenticity of the Shroud. It was as if no controversy had ever existed or would be likely in the future.

For centuries, observers of the Shroud had been able to see with the naked eye the images—both frontal and dorsal—of a man who had been beaten, crowned with thorns, gashed in his side and crucified. Although the images were vague and seemingly distorted—appearing as a series of reddish brown blotches running the length of the yellowed linen—the trained eye had little difficulty discerning what they depicted. Smaller stains of a richer color indicated the wounds and the flow of blood (see Plate 4). Some observers of the time believed that the images were impressions made by direct contact of the cloth with Christ's battered and bleeding body; others, who thought the Shroud merely an artistic representation of Christ's burial cloth, insisted that the images had been painted on. Standing outside the cathedral on that spring morning in 1898, however, was a man whose discovery of the true nature of the images would thrust the study of the Shroud into the modern world and begin a furor that has not yet ceased.

Like most of those who have dealt intimately with the Shroud, Secondo Pia was an unusual man of substantial professional accomplishments and diverse avocational pursuits. A native of the Piedmont region (of which Turin is the capital), he was born in Asti in 1855. The affluence of his family made any career possible, and he first entered the practice of law. Later, while still in his thirties, he made the almost obligatory shift, for a man of his background, into local politics. He permitted neither profession, however, to distract him from his special interests—experiments in chemistry and physics, the serious study of the region's art and culture, and an almost obsessional devotion to the then new science of photography.

Completely self-taught and something of a local pioneer in the intriguing new field, Pia had, by 1898, become a consummate technician, frequently improvising with his skills to compensate for the primitive photographic equipment available at the time. He did everything himself, from setting up his cumbersome camera to developing, mounting and framing his pictures. The one thing he never did, he often declared, was to retouch a negative.

No one knows now exactly whose idea it was for Pia to photograph the Shroud during the exposition. It is known only that he had been named to supervise a display of regional sacred art as part of the general festivities. But certainly he must have realized the importance and distinction attached to taking the first photograph of perhaps the most precious, definitely the most thought-provoking, relic known to the church. Regardless of the initial motivation, once the subject had been broached, the technical challenge alone would have compelled Pia to demonstrate his abilities.

At first Humbert I, king of Italy and nominal owner of the Shroud, opposed the photographing of it on the grounds that reproducing the sacred object in such a way would diminish the reverence and devotion accorded the relic. However, his opposition eventually dissipated, and Pia was given authorization to proceed, but only under the condition that his activities would in no way disrupt the exposition.

With today's sophisticated equipment, such restrictions would elicit perhaps no more than a fleeting shrug from a photographer, but for Pia they posed considerable problems. There were only two scheduled breaks in the proceedings that would allow sufficient time for his task.

Pia made his first attempt on the afternoon of May 25. With the aid of several helpers, he assembled a specially designed, collapsible scaffolding that would enable him to photograph the Shroud from the proper position. Floodlights diffused by ground-glass screens were used to provide adequate light. Pia planned two exposures, one of fourteen minutes and another of twenty. Yet after all his careful planning and time-consuming preparation, the heat of the lights proved too great for the glass screens, which shattered several minutes into Pia's first exposure. There was nothing to do but tear down all his equipment and wait for his second, and last available, opportunity, on the evening of the twenty-eighth.

By this time, Princess Clotilde had insisted that a special glass plate cover the Shroud to protect it from the heat of the lights. The glass would cast distracting reflections into Pia's lens. In addition, someone had stolen the bolts necessary to erect the scaffolding. Nonetheless, after two hours of preparation, Pia was ready. He was successful in obtaining both exposures without incident.

Although he had set up a temporary darkroom in the sacristy at the rear of the cathedral, Pia decided against using it, opting instead for the familiar comfort of his darkroom at home, only several minutes away.

Accounts of exactly what happened next are scarce, but the most definitive and detailed appears in *The Shroud* by John Walsh. Based on several years of extensive research, Walsh's book presents definitive reconstructions of the most important studies of the Shroud, as well as excellent portraits of most of the men central to the Shroud controversy. Here follows his account of Pia's development of his plates:

A small, red light shone feebly in Pia's darkroom as he gingerly placed the large glass plates in a solution of oxalate of iron. When the first vague outlines began to appear under the shimmering liquid, the anxiety left Pia's eyes and the frustrations of the past few days began to lift. At least there was something.

In the dim, red glare, he held the dripping plate up before his eyes. Clearly visible was the upper part of the altar with the huge frame above it containing the relic. But the brown stain-image seemed somehow different from the way it looked on the cloth itself. It had taken on a molding . . . a depth . . . a definition. Turning the plate on its side, he gazed at the face. What he saw made his hands tremble and the wet plate slipped, almost dropping to the floor. The face, with eyes closed, had become startlingly real.

"Shut up in my darkroom," Pia wrote later, "all intent on my work, I experienced a very strong emotion when, during the development, I saw for the first time the Holy Face appear on the plate, with such clarity that I was dumbfounded by it." All his life Pia was to remember that moment, speaking of it as a great glory. An emotional man under his old-fashioned reserve, his eyes were often wet after relating the details to a spellbound audience. More than once in these talks, he spoke of the "trepidation" that had seized him and made him tremble.

His first reaction to the unexpected sight in the negative, however, had been mixed with uncertainty. What he saw violated all the laws of photography and he knew it.

The stain-image, diffuse and flat on the relic, now stood out like a picture of an actual body, the contours indicated by minute gradations of shading. The face, so bizarre when viewed on the cloth, had become a harmonious, recognizable portrait of a bearded man with long hair. Emotions frozen in death emanated from the features; a vast patience, a noble resignation spoke out of the countenance. Even with the eyes shut, the face was suffused by an expression of majesty, impossible to analyze. All this on his *negative* plate [see Plate 5]!

Pia knew that in any negative there should be only a rearrangement of lights and shadows and a reversal of position. Light areas should become dark and dark areas light. Left should be right and right, left. The result should have been the usual grotesque caricature of the original that would make good sense only when printed in positive. Instead, here in his negative was a positive as real as any Pia had ever seen.

As he carefully lowered the plate into a fixative bath of hyposulphate of soda, he turned over in his mind the possible answers to the phenomenon. Had there been some kind of rare photographic accident, something never before encountered? Perhaps some strange property of lighting or camera could account for it. But Pia was an expert with a confidence born of a quarter of a century of experience; he had a sure grasp of photographic principle. He soon rejected any explanation but the obvious one: what showed on the negative was exactly what his camera had seen on the cloth. It was still dark on the morning of the twenty-ninth when he hastily wrote a short note to Baron Manno to announce the success of his undertaking. He didn't mention the unexpected discovery in this note; that news he would convey personally.

Later that morning, with a positive print made from the negative, he compared the two. There was no longer any doubt. This incredible portrait existed in the stain-image. Although to the naked eye the brownish stains on the relic presented only haphazard outlines, they must, in reality, form a negative, or at least they must possess, in some mysterious way, the qualities of a negative. Thus, when a picture is taken of the cloth, and the negative plate developed, the stain-image is reversed in light values and relative position and shows positive characteristics. Exactly the same process would occur if a picture were taken of a real photographic negative.

25

As dawn crept through the streets of Turin, Pia sat before the negative and its print, occupied with a sudden, stunning thought. No human being could have painted this negative that lies hidden in the stains. . . . If it was not painted, not made by human hands, then . . . gazing fixedly, Pia felt a numbing certitude that he was looking on the face of Jesus.

Before Secondo Pia's remarkable discovery, of those who knew of or had seen the Shroud, believers had believed and skeptics had scoffed. But since the Shroud had been exposed to view so infrequently during the almost six hundred years of its documented existence, there had been little reasonable basis for any position. The earlier squabbles about where the Shroud had originated and what it really was seem to have been conducted on a somewhat lofty plane within the church hierarchy, with little impact on the public at large.

Pia's photograph changed all that, and the world press had a field day with the story. Requests for copies of the photograph flooded in, and investigative work by scholars and scientists began in earnest. For his part, Pia was for a time attacked and vilified as the perpetrator of a cruel and sacrilegious hoax. Finally he was upheld.

It seemed that neither the church nor the House of Savoy wanted the publicity or the controversy. At the end of the exposition, on June 2, 1898, the Shroud was immediately returned to its silver casket and stored in its triple-locked crypt. All requests for its further examination were either denied or ignored. The Shroud would not again see the light of day until 1931.

# II

## What the Shroud Is

The Shroud of Turin does exist. It is a long strip of cloth, of which the most commonly agreed upon measure is 14 feet, 3 inches long, and 3 feet, 7 inches wide. (The fact that even its dimensions have been contested is but another example of how restricted access to it has been.) Although the cloth is creased and yellowed with age, it is still supple and, for the most part, well preserved. It is made of pure linen, woven in a herringbone pattern in what is referred to as a three-to-one twill: that is, the weft, or horizontal, thread passes alternately over three and under one of the warp, or vertical, threads (see Plate 3).

According to Virginio Timossi, the textile expert who examined it in 1931, the Shroud bears many signs of having been manufactured in a primitive way, as there are irregularities in the pattern and imperfections in the weave. Dr. William Geilmann, another textile authority and a professor at the University of Mainz, Germany, has been able to demonstrate and authenticate a number of similar linen fabrics, all of which reliably date from the first to the third century. One of Dr. Geilmann's fabrics is woven in exactly the same pattern as that of the Shroud of Turin.

Weaving of this sort has been traced back to early Egyptian times, and similar cloths have been found which date from as far back as 1500 B.C. Some of the cloths found in the tombs of King Sethos I (circa 1300 B.C.), Ramses III (1200 B.C.) and Queen Makeri (1100 B.C.) are woven in the same three-to-one twill pattern. It is said that the Jews learned the art of weaving from the Egyptians during their captivity, and that they practiced the craft so well that Jewish cloth was often preferred to the Egyptian.

In Palestine itself, no cloth is known to have been preserved, owing to the extreme humidity of climate. Burial shrouds in Palestine would normally have been destroyed quickly by the decomposition of the bodies they covered. In Egypt, however, the mummification of the body, and the application of numerous bandages and wrappings, have ensured the preservation of some funeral cloths. Cloths resembling the Shroud and dating from the Greco-Roman period have been preserved at Dura-Europos in Syria.

There is no evidence to the contrary that linen of this kind was in fact in common use in Palestine at the time of Christ; but the material alone cannot date the Shroud conclusively to that time since the use of twill weaves spanned so many centuries. Neither is there any evidence that the twill weave was used in France either shortly before or during the fourteenth century, when the Shroud turned up there—and this poses severe obstructions to the arguments of some critics that the Shroud was a forgery of that period.

The most striking—and disconcerting—feature of the Shroud is the double line of black spots and white triangles which run the length of the cloth.

The black spots and lines are the traces of a fire which burned down the Holy Chapel of Chambéry, France, in 1532, nearly destroying the Shroud. It was kept folded in a silver casket, from which a drop of molten metal fell, burning the cloth in a symmetrical pattern. The white triangles are patches sewn on to replace areas that were completely consumed. In addition, a pattern of lozenge-shaped stains is faintly visible, the remains of water that was thrown on the relic to extinguish the fire. Repairs were made by the Poor Clares (nuns) of Chambéry, who also sewed a piece of cloth onto the back of the Shroud. This was replaced during the nineteenth century by Princess Clotilde of Italy, who, it is said, sewed every stitch with her own hands and never rose from her knees while fulfilling the task.

Two groups of small, dark circles, visible especially at the level of the loins on the dorsal image, suggest a burning that took place under different circumstances. Since these are reproduced on a copy of the Shroud executed in 1516 and attributed to Albrecht Dürer, the indication is that the Shroud must have been involved in another, earlier fire of which there is no record. There is, however, one other interpretation of these markings as we will see in a subsequent chapter.

Between the two lines of burns and patches are two images of a human body, one frontal and one dorsal. The length of the frontal image is 6.7257 feet; the dorsal, 6.8596 feet. The difference is slightly greater than an inch and a half, and can be explained by the effects of rigor mortis pulling the chin toward the chest, thus slightly reducing the length of the frontal image. The two images lie head to head, separated by a space which, while bearing no signs of any image, would approximate the size of the crown of a man's head. A sixteenth-century painting by the artist Clovio depicts the manner in which the Shroud must have been wrapped lengthwise around the body for the images to have been formed in this way (see Plate 1).

The stains that make up the images are of two distinctly different types and colors: the bloodstains are a rich carmine in color; the stains which comprise the images of the body are sepia-toned. On the Shroud itself, the bloodstains appear as positive images, while the body appears as a negative. On the negative photograph, the body appears as positive, while the bloodstains take on negative characteristics. The implication of this disparity is that the two types of stains were transferred onto the cloth in different ways: the bloodstains by direct contact, and the body images by some sort of projection.

The images of the body are formed by continuous, mistlike stains which completely penetrate the thread of the fabric. According to the testimony of the Poor Clares, the imprints appear on the reverse side of the Shroud with almost equal clarity. There are no sharp lines of demarcation; at the edges of the images the color gradually fades away. The delicate shading of the imprints allows the observer to discern, with some clarity, the contours of the body. Protruding masses leave a dark imprint, while depressions, hollows and crevices are indicated by a much lighter coloration. The subtlety of the images becomes much more apparent on the negative photograph than on the actual Shroud.

The face on the frontal image is reproduced with

particular clarity (see Plate 8). The hair, the mustache, the beard, the orbital ridges, the nose and the lips stand out quite distinctly. The left side of the face (left of subject, but also left of observer looking at the negative photograph because of the image reversal principle of photography) made a much heavier imprint than the right and, in the negative photograph, looks swollen, as though it had been struck. Traces of blows are also visible on the nose and upper lip. The mustache and mouth are twisted slightly to the right, presumably because the cloth was not evenly applied to the face. On the whole, however, it may be stated that the face, as seen in the negative, is reproduced with very little distortion.

Streaks of blood are noticeable on the forehead and in the hair. One such streak is traceable to a sharp puncture, which is faithfully reproduced. Similar streaks of blood appear on the neck of the dorsal image (see Plate 16).

The shoulders and neck of the body have left no trace on the frontal imprint, suggesting that the head was bent forward and held in position by rigor mortis. The contours of the chest and stomach appear clearly, as do the forearms and hands, which are crossed over the groin, obscuring the genital region (see Plate 11). The delicacy of the shading allows the observer to distinguish each finger, but on both hands the thumbs are obviously missing. This may seem odd at first, but as we shall later see, the missing thumbs are of the utmost importance to the authenticity of the Shroud.

On the left side of the rib cage is a heavy stain thought to represent a gaping wound (see Plate 14). From this wound there was a copious flow of abnormally thick blood, such as might issue from a corpse. A clear, organic fluid also ran from this wound, and has left a faint stain that extends beyond the edges of the blood flow.

On the right wrist, there is a heavy bloodstain, obviously caused by a major wound. A trickle of blood runs from the wound up the right forearm. The left wrist is obscured by the right hand, which overlaps it, but there is a similar trickle of blood running up the left forearm, indicating a wound on the left wrist as well.

On the dorsal image, the back, buttocks and thighs are covered with streaks of blood which fall into a roughly regular pattern (see Plate 17). The blood appears to have clotted over excoriations such as might have been caused by severe scourging. In many cases, the wounds inflicted by the bits of bone or lead lodged in the thongs of Roman whips can be seen quite clearly. Traces of severe abrasions appear in the region of the shoulders (see Plate 16).

The direction of the blood flow in most cases suggests that the body was in an upright position when wounded, and for some time thereafter. The blood from the wrist wounds indicates that the arms were extended and bent at two different angles to the body, as would be the case of a man hanging from a cross, alternately lifting himself and letting himself hang (see Plate 10).

In the somewhat unclear region of the feet, the wound on the left foot is seen more clearly on the dorsal than on the frontal image.

In various places on the imprints appear stains left by small drops of serous fluid which exuded from the pores of the body; such serum flows from a corpse.

There is no trace anywhere on the Shroud of putrefaction, indicating that the body must have been removed from the Shroud before decomposition began to damage the cloth.

In later chapters we will explore exactly how this mysterious two-thousand-year-old "photograph" with its medically accurate physical properties could have come to be, but it is first necessary to clearly establish the known history of the Shroud and to deal with the archaeological questions of its origin.

# III

## The Testament of the Gospels

Writing in the *New Catholic Encyclopedia,* the Reverend Adam J. Otterbein, a Redemptorist priest and president of the Holy Shroud Guild of Esopus, New York, states, "If the Shroud of Turin is authentic, the imprints of the body must concur with the details of the Gospel account of the Passion." This attitude has influenced virtually every reasonable historical study of the Shroud, pro or con, that has been conducted, and immense exegetical effort has gone into establishing or refuting such corroboration.

There is, in fact, a substantial case for arguing that the origin of the Shroud and its markings do not violate Gospel descriptions, as we shall see. But we must accept the fact that the Gospels *as we know them* are controversial in both form and content, regardless of their original veracity and historical accuracy, and regardless of our own religious beliefs. Of dubious authorship, corrupted by copyists, with possible parts missing and others out of place, misinterpreted in translation, perhaps censored, lacking in critical detail and presenting disparities among themselves, the Gospels are at best faulty records of the origin of Christianity generally and of the Shroud specifically. Nonetheless, they are the only records we have, and must therefore be taken seriously and studied diligently. But where there are, or seem to be, conflicts between the texts of the Gospels and the authenticity of the Shroud, then neither can take precedence over the other without considerable external evidence.

Because of their similarities in content, order and statement, the first three Gospels—those attributed to the evangelists Matthew, Mark and Luke, and dated between A.D. 65 and 135—are commonly referred to as the Synoptics. As such, they present a reasonably unified account of the Passion.

For the purposes of this book, I shall recount only those parts that have relevance to the Shroud, paraphrasing from the translation of The New English Bible. Points of particular importance are italicized for emphasis.

On Friday morning following Jesus' "trial," when Pontius Pilate had finally concluded that nothing short of Jesus' death would satisfy the chief priests and elders, *he had Jesus flogged and handed him over to be crucified.* Pilate's soldiers stripped Jesus and dressed him in a scarlet (or purple) mantle. *A crown of thorns was placed on his head,* and a cane in his right hand. He was jeered, spat upon and *beaten about the head with the cane.* When the soldiers had finished their mockery and abuse, the mantle was removed and Jesus was again dressed in his own clothes. Then he was led away to be crucified. *On the way, Simon of Cyrene was pressed into service to carry the cross.*

Arriving at Golgotha, the place of crucifixion, *Jesus was "fastened" to the cross (or "was cruci-*

fied"), and was further abused. The hour of crucifixion was nine o'clock in the morning. From midday
until about three in the afternoon, a darkness fell
over the whole land. At about three o'clock, Jesus
cried out, and a bystander offered him a sponge
soaked with sour wine, which he held to Jesus' lips
at the end of a cane (or short javelin). Jesus
again gave a loud cry, and died.

*It was the day before the Sabbath,* and when
evening came, Joseph of Arimathaea, a wealthy disciple, approached Pilate and requested the body of
Jesus. Pilate was surprised that Jesus was already
dead, but after establishing that fact, he decreed
that Joseph should have the body. *Joseph took the
body down from the cross, wrapped it in a clean
linen cloth which he had bought, and placed it in his
own unused tomb, which had been cut out of rock.*
He then rolled a large stone against the entrance
and left. Mary of Magdala and Mary the mother of
Joseph were watching and saw where Jesus was
laid.

On Saturday, the Sabbath, the chief priests and
Pharisees asked Pilate to place a guard on the tomb
so that Jesus' disciples could not steal the body away
and then claim he had risen from the dead as he
had prophesied. The tomb was sealed and a guard
was left in charge.

*Early on Sunday morning, after the Sabbath was
over, a group of women went to the tomb with
spices, oils and perfumes in order to anoint Jesus'
body.* When they arrived, they found that the stone
had been rolled away and Jesus was gone.

Although somewhat vague and sketchy, nothing
more than an outline really, that is the essence of

events as revealed in the Synoptics. As we explore them detail for detail, we will see that they present no significant obstacle to the authenticity of the Shroud. But first we must examine the Gospel of John. Again, important points are italicized.

Of the four Gospels, that of John is generally considered the most controversial and also the most troublesome as it concerns the Shroud, although it does contain some important additional details not mentioned in the Synoptics. Reputed to have been written by the Galilean fisherman and one of the earliest and dearest disciples, the Fourth Gospel differs in many respects from the Synoptics. Because of the numerous discrepancies, there is considerable doubt that John the Apostle was actually the author. That question, however, is a matter for other books. Our task is to ascertain what bearing the text we have, whoever the author, has on the Shroud.

To the account of the Synoptics, John adds the important detail that the Friday of the crucifixion was not only the eve of the Sabbath, but of Passover as well.

Where the Synoptics merely say that Pilate's soldiers beat Jesus about the head, John is more specific, recounting that they *struck him on the face.*

John's description of the time of crucifixion would seem to make it somewhat later than the hour fixed by the Synoptics, since, according to John, Pilate did not send Jesus away to be crucified until noon.

John specifically says that *Jesus carried his own cross.*

Following Jesus' death, John describes the blow with the lance, unmentioned by the Synoptics:

Because it was the eve of Passover, the Jews were anxious that the bodies should not remain on the cross for the coming Sabbath, since that Sabbath was a day of great solemnity; so they requested Pilate to have the legs broken [to hasten death] and the bodies taken down. The soldiers accordingly came to the first of his fellow victims and to the second, and broke their legs; but when they came to Jesus, they found that he was already dead, so they did not break his legs. *But one of the soldiers stabbed his side with a lance, and at once there was a flow of blood and water.*

John's description of the burial is as follows:

After that, Pilate was approached by Joseph of Arimathaea, a disciple of Jesus, but a secret disciple for fear of the Jews, who asked to be allowed to remove the body of Jesus. Pilate gave the permission; so Joseph came and took the body away. He was joined by Nicodemus . . . who brought with him *a mixture of myrrh and aloes, more than half a hundredweight. They took the body of Jesus and wrapped it, with the spices, in strips of linen cloth according to Jewish burial customs.* Now at the place where he had been crucified there was a garden, and in the garden a new tomb, not yet used for burial. *There, because the tomb was near at hand and it was the eve of the Jewish Sabbath, they laid Jesus.*

Here is John's account of the events of Sunday morning:

Early on the Sunday morning, while it was still dark, Mary of Magdala came to the tomb. She saw that the stone had been moved away from the entrance, and ran to Simon Peter and the other disciple, the one whom Jesus loved. "They have taken the Lord out of his tomb," she cried, "and we do not know where they have laid him." So Peter and the other set out and made their way to the tomb. They were running side by side, but the other disciple outran Peter and reached the tomb first. *He peered in and saw the linen wrappings lying there,* but did not enter. Then Simon Peter came up, following him, and he went into the tomb. *He saw the linen wrappings lying, and the napkin which had been over his head, not lying with the wrappings but rolled together in a place by itself.* Then the disciple who had reached the tomb first went in too, and he saw and believed; until then they had not understood the Scriptures, which showed that he must rise from the dead.

Later on Sunday, in the evening, eleven of the disciples were together in a room when Jesus came to them. *He showed them "his hands and his side."* The twelfth disciple, Thomas, was not present, and when the others told him they had seen Jesus, he did not believe them.

He said, "Unless I see the mark of the nails on his hands, unless I put my finger into the place where the nails were, and my hand into his side, I will not believe it."

A week later his disciples were again in the room, and Thomas was with them. Although the doors were locked, Jesus came and stood among them, saying, "Peace be with you!" *Then he said to Thomas, "Reach your finger here; see my hands. Reach your hand here and put it into my side.* Be unbelieving no longer, but believe." Thomas said, "My Lord and my God!" Jesus said, "Because you have seen me you have found faith. Happy are they who never saw me and yet have found faith."

(Of the Synoptics, only Luke mentions this episode, and then only vaguely; John's account is much more detailed.)

Using the four Gospel accounts as the framework for our analysis, we must now compare them, point by point, with the images and markings on the Shroud, supplementing our knowledge with additional historical information not detailed in the Gospels.

## The Flogging

According to Matthew (27:26), Mark (15:15) and John (19:12), Jesus was severely scourged, or flogged, at the praetorium before setting out for Golgotha. In Luke (27:18, 23), Pilate twice attempted to have Jesus let off with the flogging as his only punishment, but Luke does not specifically refer to the flogging as having actually taken place.

Markings on the Shroud reveal the wounds of the flogging to be in great number, at least one hundred, perhaps more. Shaped like tiny barbells, the contusions cover the entire image of the body, from the shoulders to the lower part of the legs, most of them appearing on the dorsal image (see Plate 18).

In addition to having been a general punishment in and of itself, flogging seems to have been a customary accompaniment to any execution, regardless of the final method of death—usually crucifixion, impalement or beheading. Prior to execution, the victim was stripped, his hands tied in front of him to an upright stake or column, and he was whipped from behind. Sometimes he was also whipped on his way to the place of execution. Jewish law forbade administering more than forty lashes, and the Pharisees had reduced the number to thirty-nine. Among the Romans no such restraint, short of death, is known to have applied; and we can be certain that many did die, if not immediately, then later, from either infection or internal hemorrhaging. The evidence of the Shroud indicates that Jesus was struck excessively.

The Gospels describe the scourging with the technical term *flagellare*—"to whip." From the details of the wounds as seen on the Shroud, it is quite clear that in the case of Jesus the flogging was carried out with the *flagellum*, or, more likely, with the larger and heavier *flagrum* (see Plate 19). These dread instruments of punishment consisted of short handles to which several long thongs or chains were attached. Near the striking ends of the thongs, bits of bone or lumps of lead were affixed, their sole purpose to bite deeply into the flesh of the naked victim, weakening him and reducing his resistance to the ordeal to come.

The *flagrum* was a brutal device, so abhorrent that it was not used on Roman citizens or, generally, on free men. For them, the *virga,* the rod or switch were reserved by law. But Jesus was treated as an outcast and criminal of the lowest order. And once Pilate had ceremoniously washed his hands of the whole affair, it is no great wonder that the best Jesus was to receive was the worst that the Romans could conceive.

41

## The Crown of Thorns

One of the most extensive studies of crucifixion and its attendant circumstances was undertaken by the Reverend U. Holzmeister, and published in 1934 in *Verbum Domini,* the review of the Pontifical Biblical Institute, under the title "Crux Domini eiusque crucifixio ex archaeologia romana illustrantur." Holzmeister believed that ridicule was obligatory to a Roman crucifixion, and that the crown of thorns—along with the dressing of Jesus in fine garments, the placing of the cane in his hand and the verbal mockery—was an example of this.

Unfortunately, Holzmeister's fragmentary sources do not conclusively prove his case, and it is difficult to believe that such elaborate proceedings were the rule of the day. Regardless of the excesses we might wish to attribute to the Romans, crucifixions were just too common and too routinely handled for such elaborate displays to have taken place with all but the most exceptional victims. At any rate, the crown of thorns, as far as can be determined, was a unique feature of the crucifixion of Jesus.

Again, Matthew (27:29), Mark (15:18) and John (19:2) attest that the crowning actually took place—"Plaiting a crown of thorns they placed it on his head." Luke is silent on the subject.

On the Shroud, bloodstains encircle the image of the head. It is generally believed by those who have studied the Shroud that the crown of thorns was not the circlet or wreath-shaped headband so frequently depicted in Christian art, but was rather shaped like a cap or helmet and covered the entire head, with plaited rushes securing it under the chin (see Plate

9). Thorns said to have come from the crown exist throughout the world and have been venerated by Christians for centuries. Although impossible to authenticate, they belong to a type of lotebush common in Judea, and are long and sharp—quite capable of having produced the abundant flow of blood which appears on the Shroud.

## The Beating About Jesus' Head

All four Gospels are in accord that Jesus underwent several series of beatings prior to crucifixion (Matthew 26:67–68, 27:31; Mark 14:65, 15:19; Luke 22:63–64; John 19:3). Fists and a cane or stick were used, and the blows were aimed specifically at his head or face.

Medical authorities, most notably Dr. Pierre Barbet, have noted that the markings on the Shroud show a large bruise on the right cheek and other evidence to indicate that Jesus' nose was broken.

## Crucifixion

The origins of crucifixion and the extent to which it was used as a means of execution in antiquity are unclear. Most authorities believe that the Persians practiced crucifixion regularly; but this assertion is based on the testimony of Greek authors, Herodotus in particular, and the practices of the Persians are referred to with verbs (*anastauroun* and *anaskolopizein*) that could easily refer to impalement on a pointed stake rather than specifically to crucifixion. Darius I of Persia (521–486 B.C.), speaking in the Behistun inscription of the execution of his enemies, used an expression that is usually translated "I impaled." Impalement was common in the ancient Near East, particularly among the Assyrians, who depicted it in their triumphal reliefs.

It is often said that the Greeks before Alexander the Great recoiled from crucifixion, but Herodotus states that during the Persian Wars (490–479 B.C.), Greeks crucified Artayctes, the Persian governor of Sestos. In describing the event, Herodotus does not use the suspect verbs mentioned above. On the contrary, his language is prophetic of things to come: "They nailed him alive to a plank. . . . Having nailed him to a plank, they hung him up."

There is little doubt that crucifixion was widely practiced in the Hellenistic monarchies of the Near East, by the Phoenicians, and in Carthage. Among the Romans, crucifixion, as we understand it, seems to have been introduced at the time of the Punic Wars in the third century B.C., and was thought of as a punishment applicable primarily to slaves. A master had absolute power over his slaves, and severe punishment could be, and was, meted out for the most trivial reasons. It was administered with special rigor, and by the state, in the case of slaves who had revolted. When the slave insurrection led by Spartacus was quelled in 71 B.C., six thousand crosses lined the road from Capua to Rome.

Pirates, bandits and rebellious subjects of the Roman Empire were also punished with crucifixion. Vivid examples of the latter category are recorded in Judea. The legate Quintilius Varus, having put down a rebellion which followed the death of Herod the Great in the year 3 B.C., crucified two thousand of its leaders. During the siege of Jerusalem in A.D. 69, those who were caught trying to make their escape from the city were crucified in full sight of its walls. The executions often exceeded five hundred per day, and it is said that the soldiers amused themselves by varying the positions in which the condemned were attached to their crosses.

The crucifixion of Roman citizens was regarded as an outrage. In 201 B.C., Scipio Africanus crucified the Roman deserters handed over to him by the Carthaginians, and both Livy and Valerius Maximus record the horror over this act. Cicero's catalogue of the atrocities committed by Verres, the Roman governor of Sicily, culminates in the description of the unjust and cruel punishments inflicted by him, and this mass of horrors is in turn crowned by a dramatic account of the crucifixion of a man who claimed to be a Roman citizen.

Crucifixion seems to have been regarded as the most painful and the most ignominious form of capital punishment. Its use was discontinued by Constantine, the first Christian emperor, in about A.D. 314.

## The Cross

The Roman cross consisted of two parts: an upright stake fixed in the ground (*palus, stipes*), and a transverse beam (*patibulum*). The stake always stood outside the city walls; in Rome, a whole forest of crosses stood outside the Esquiline gate.

Some Shroud scholars have debated whether the cross of Jesus was high or low. That some crosses of the period were low may be inferred from a number of references to the devouring of the bodies of the crucified by wild beasts, but that at least one cross in Roman history was a high one is clear from an anecdote in Suetonius' *Life of Galba:* When a man who had been condemned to the cross protested that he was a Roman citizen, Galba, the Roman emperor in A.D. 69, ordered that a high and whitewashed cross be prepared for him.

The Gospels do not refer to the size of the cross on which Jesus was mounted, but they do say that as he was hanging a sponge was held up to his lips at the end of a cane or stick (Matthew 27:48; Mark 15:26) or on the point of a javelin (John 19:29).

It seems useless to argue on the basis of the Gospel passages that the cross was either high or low. Certainly something would have been used to pass the sponge to Jesus in either case. Those present at the crucifixion were not strangers to the phenomenon. They knew what the ordeal did to a man, and no one in his senses would bring his hands near the mouth of a man in the grip of severe convulsions for fear of having his fingers bitten off.

The external evidence suggests that the cross was usually low, and there is nothing in the Gospels to indicate that the crucifixion of Jesus was exceptional in this respect. The point is significant only as it concerns the piercing of Jesus' side by the lance; and although medical men disagree, it is extremely doubtful that the evidence will ever be firm enough to fully support any viewpoint.

The controversy, no matter how slight, does help to point out the complexities of dealing with the Shroud, particularly in light of the slight, fragmentary and often contradictory textual and archaeological evidence with which we must deal.

Some crosses were equipped with a projecting peg (*sedile*), which was straddled by the condemned man. This is mentioned only by late, but pre-Constantinian, authors Justin and Tertullian, who refer specifically to the crucifixion of Jesus. Though not shown specifically in Christian art, this seems to be a matter of reverence more than concern for fact.

At some point in time, with some crucifixions, the footrest, or *suppedaneum,* might also have been appended to the cross. The earliest mention of this is in the Middle Ages, although it has been discerned by some authorities to have appeared in the third-century Palatine graffito, a satirical wall-drawing mocking a Christian named Alexamenos.

The purpose of the *sedile* and *suppedaneum* would have been to support the crucified man, thus reducing the weight on the nails through the wrists and prolonging his suffering. Origen wrote that the crucified often lived through the night and the following day, and Eusebius contended that the victims of the cross died of hunger. Neither statement can be true of all crucifixions, but they can be taken as indications that the agonies on the cross were often prolonged. The fact that Pilate was surprised when he was told that Jesus had died after only a few hours on the cross might indicate that some sort of support was indeed common and was used on Jesus' cross, but that is a very flimsy argument in support of this contention.

The condemned were sometimes tied with rope to their crosses, but it was more customary to nail them. In Greek, to "nail up" means to crucify. Nails were driven through the victim's wrists and feet, although it is a matter of some controversy whether the feet were secured together with one nail or separately. The most compelling evidence, however, based on medical examinations of the Shroud and on a recent archaeological find, is in favor of the one nail.

Of the crucifixion itself, the Gospels only say that Jesus was "fastened" to the cross (Matthew 27:35; Mark 15:24) or that he "was crucified" (Luke 23:33; John 19:18). There are no details, no specifics; yet if anything at all is certain about the Shroud, it is that the man represented on it was crucified with nails through his wrists and feet (see Plate 7). The wounds are there for all to see. They are startling in their reality, and there can be no confusion as to what they are.

## The Carrying of the Cross

When the Greeks spoke of "carrying a cross," they undoubtedly meant carrying a part of the cross, namely the *patibulum,* or crossbeam. Latin sources mention only the *patibulum.* The procedure is alluded to, but not clearly described in Jesus' prophetic words to Peter (John 21:18–19): " '. . . when you were young you fastened your belt about you and walked where you chose; but when you are old, you will stretch out your arms, and a stranger will bind you fast and carry you where you have no wish to go.' He said this to indicate the manner of death [crucifixion] by which Peter was to glorify God."

Most of the extant references to the fact that condemned men were forced to carry their own crosses concern slaves. A slave, naked and bearing his *patibulum,* was whipped through the most public places of the city on his way to execution. The *patibulum* was placed across his shoulders, and his

wrists were tied to its extremities, although Diony-
sius of Halicarnassus speaks of a beam laid across the
chest and shoulders of the condemned man.

Of Jesus, we are told that he "took up his own
cross" (John 19:17), and also that it was carried for
him by Simon of Cyrene (Matthew 27:32; Mark
15:21; Luke 23:26). The Gospels are again silent
on details, but here we can at least make some
reasonable assumptions in piecing together the story
and reconciling the Gospel accounts. Jesus probably
did begin carrying the cross, as was customary, but
owing to his weakened condition from the flogging
and beatings and to the ruggedness of the terrain, he
fell frequently, and the movement toward Golgotha
was exceptionally slow and tedious. Because of the
approaching Passover Sabbath, everyone wanted the
crucifixion to be done with as soon as possible, and
thus Simon was enlisted to carry the cross the remainder of the way.

In an effort to verify this contention, Monsignor
Giulio Ricci, a Vatican archivist who has spent
twenty years studying the complexities of the
Shroud, attempted to duplicate the walk of Christ
aided by a hired man. Unlike Jesus, the man was fit
and healthy, but in simulating the journey he fell so
many times that the experiment had to be stopped
before they reached Golgotha.

On the Shroud, across the image of the right
shoulder is a mass of tiny lacerations that indicate to
medical authorities they were caused by a rough,
heavy object chafing that shoulder—an object that
was almost certainly a crossbeam. In addition,
wounds in other places give evidence of numerous
falls along a rocky path.

## The Blow with the Lance

Of the Gospels, John (19:31–37) alone refers to the important detail of the lance thrust. Because the Jews did not want the bodies of Jesus and his two companions to remain on their crosses during the Passover Sabbath, they asked Pilate to have their legs broken and the bodies removed from the crosses.

The Latin term for this breaking of the shins following crucifixion is *crurifragium*. Its purpose was exactly opposite that of the *sedile* and the *suppedaneum*. While they were specifically designed to prolong the victim's life and agony on the cross, the *crurifragium* would assure a rapid death by bringing on tetany and asphyxia.

From the references of Seneca, Ammiañus Marcellinus, Origen and Plautus, we can be reasonably certain that *crurifragium* was a common practice in and around Rome. But Jesus was already dead, so there was no need for his legs to be broken. Instead, one of the soldiers pierced his side with a lance. Why?

Usually the victims of crucifixion were left on their crosses to be devoured by wild beasts or birds of prey, or simply to rot. According to a Roman law of the imperial period, however, it was possible for the families of the deceased to obtain the bodies for decent burial. In such cases, a single reference of antiquity suggests that the executioners were required by law to administer a sort of *coup de grâce* to the crucified—even when they were apparently already dead—before giving over the remains to the mourners. Quintilian, an author of the first century, writes: "Crosses [or the crucified] are cut down, and the executioner does not forbid the burial of those who have been smitten [or pierced, presumably with a sword or javelin]."

Origen, in the Latin translation of his *Commentary on Matthew,* says that the lance thrust was administered "according to Roman custom, below the armpit." Such a blow would correspond exactly with the location of the wound in the side as seen on the Shroud (see Plate 14). That wound resembles an elongated oval and is 1¾ inches by 7⁄16 of an inch. These dimensions indicate an incision made by the *lancea* in common usage by Roman auxiliaries— a spear with a long, leaflike tip that rounded off toward the shaft. From the wound of the lance, a massive flow of blood is evident on the Shroud—a large, dark stain intermingled with smaller, clear stains—the "water" attested to by John.

## The Shroud and the Burial

So far there have been no significant conflicts between the markings on the Shroud and the relevant Gospel passages. Neither the Shroud nor the Gospels violates the archaeological framework, scant though it is, into which they must be placed. If we had only the Synoptics with which to contend, such would be the case throughout the remainder of this discussion. But as we arrive at the two most crucial points of the Gospel narratives—their specific references to the Shroud and their accounts of the actual disposition of Christ's body—John's text, as well as what we know of Jewish burial customs, presents problems.

In the Old Testament, burial was regarded as a matter of the utmost importance. One was expected to bury even strangers and enemies; failure to do so was considered a sign of great wickedness. Bodies were either interred in graves dug into the ground or placed in tombs hollowed out of rock. Rock tombs generally had shelves or troughs in the shape of coffins along the walls. This is suggested in the Old Testament and confirmed by the archaeology of Palestine.

There is every reason to believe that burial took place as soon as possible after death, preferably on the same day. Even corpses of criminals who had been suspended from trees were taken down before sunset and buried. It was, and still is, customary in the Middle East to bury as quickly as possible because of the rapid decomposition of bodies in the extreme heat. The Jews considered a dead body polluting to the touch, and, as with other of their laws, their religious strictures on the subject were firmly based on practical codes of health and hygiene.

In the Old Testament, Jacob and Joseph were, as important personages in Egypt, mummified in the Egyptian manner. Embalming or other preparations for the tomb are not otherwise mentioned in the Old Testament, and Palestinian archaeology has revealed no mummies. According to the Mishnah, the body of Jewish law first codified by Rabbi Judah in about A.D. 200, a body was washed and anointed as the first step of burial. Present-day analogies suggest that the washing was done with warm, perfumed water, though there is no evidence in the literature. Neither is there any indication of what ointments were used or exactly how the anointing was performed.

In the Old Testament, the mighty were buried with the garments, ornaments and weapons that had belonged to them in life. By the time the Mishnah was compiled, many considered obligatory a raiment so sumptuous that dying people were often abandoned by their relatives, thus leaving the trouble and expense of the funeral to the community at large. This abuse was rebuked by the examples set by Rabbis Gamaliel and Judah, who bade their heirs inter them in simple linen sheets. Linen garments were generally spoken of in connection with the funerals of the humble.

The chin of the deceased was held in place by a chin band, and although nothing is said in the rabbinical literature of tying the hands and feet with thongs or bands, it may by safely assumed that this practical necessity was also common. Only in the Mishnah do we hear of the covering of the face with a handkerchief; it is there stated that this had formerly been the practice of the poor, whose faces had been made unsightly by their privations, but the rule had become generalized. Here, as elsewhere in the Mishnah, it is difficult to apply a time-frame to the information given, but it is safe to assume that the practice was free and fluid by the time of Jesus' death. Whatever garments were worn to the tomb, and however they were arranged, the face of the deceased was not generally concealed by them. Even the most ascetic rabbis who were buried in simple sheets probably wore these sheets draped around their bodies, as they had done in life. Whether in splendor or in simplicity, Jews were buried dressed and not shrouded. The handkerchief over the face was at first optional and later mandatory, but the main garment was never draped over the head.

Thus, if Jesus did receive the complete and customary ritual burial, the Shroud of Turin could not possibly be the true burial cloth, for there are two absolute imperatives to the Shroud's authenticity in that respect: First, the burial cloth of Christ must have been a large, single sheet of linen that was wrapped lengthwise around the body, from head to foot. It could not have been arranged like a garment. Second, the burial must have been provisional and temporary rather than complete. If it had been complete, and the body thus washed and anointed according to custom, there would have been little, if any, blood left on the body to be transferred by direct contact onto the Shroud.

Let us now, once again, pick up the Gospel chronology. The Synoptics (Matthew 27:57–61; Mark 15:42–47; Luke 23:50–56) are unanimous concerning the key elements of what happened: Joseph of Arimathaea petitioned Pilate for Christ's body so that it might be buried. Receiving permission after some delay, Joseph wrapped the body in a clean linen sheet (Mark says he bought it specifically for the purpose), and laid it in a new, unused tomb that was cut out of rock (Matthew says it was Joseph's own tomb). Mary of Magdala and Mary the mother of Joseph followed him and saw where and how Jesus was entombed.

(To have played such an unusual and important part in the story of Christ, Joseph of Arimathaea is a shadowy figure about whom little is known. Undoubtedly he was a rich Jew, probably a member of the Sanhedrin, the highest religious and secular council of his people. A secret disciple, he had attempted to protect Jesus from his fate before boldly declaring his faith following the crucifixion. It is ironic, if not apocryphal, that this man who was responsible for providing the Shroud is also credited —by medieval legend—with carrying the Holy Grail to England in about A.D. 64, and founding the first Christian church in that country.)

The ancient Greek word used by the Synoptics for the burial cloth is *sindon,* which means precisely a sheet of linen. *Sindon* can also be used generally to designate a single strip of linen used for any purpose: a sheet, a garment, a sail, and so forth. Its modern Greek descendant, *sendoni,* means bedsheet. It is from *sindon* that the word for study of the Shroud—sindonology—is derived.

Several non-biblical texts use *sindon* in a funerary context, referring to it as the outer wrapping of a mummy. In its only other occurrence in the New Testament (Mark 14:51), it describes a garment, a sheet draped around the body like a robe. It also appears with the same meaning in a recently revealed paragraph that was either interpolated into Mark's Gospel after it was written or, as some believe, was originally written by Mark and later suppressed. In that paragraph, brought to light by the controversial *Clement of Alexandria and a Secret Gospel of Mark* by Morton Smith, a young man was initiated into the mysteries of the kingdom of God in an all-night ceremony wearing nothing but a sindon.

The Synoptics' use of the word *sindon* is thus clear and accurate, with no ambiguities: Jesus was wrapped or enfolded in a large, single sheet of linen. The Shroud of Turin is a large, single sheet of linen.

Regarding the burial, the Synoptics are equally simple and direct: Joseph wrapped the body in the linen sheet and laid it in a tomb cut out of rock. That is all they say about it. There is no mention that the body was washed. There is no mention that it was anointed. There are no details to support a complete ritual burial.

What we *are* told is that Mary of Magdala and Mary the mother of Joseph were watching and saw where and how Jesus was laid. On the Sabbath they rested. But, following the Sabbath, very early on Sunday morning, a larger group of women returned to the tomb, bringing with them spices, oils and perfumes, *intending to anoint the remains* (Matthew 28:1; Mark 16:1; Luke 24:1). If the burial had been complete, there would have been no reason for the women to return, and certainly not with the intention of anointing the body.

Thus the Synoptics offer every indication of a temporary burial, with Jesus wrapped in a large, single linen sheet.

John is at one with the Synoptics in stressing the lateness of the hour and the haste with which the burial was performed because of the approaching Sabbath (John 19:31). By his account, however, not everything was done by Joseph; Nicodemus appeared on the scene, bringing with him a mixture of myrrh and aloes. They then "took the body of Jesus and wrapped it, with the spices, in strips of linen cloth according to Jewish burial customs" (John 19:38–42).

The New English Bible translation of the above passage is open to many objections. "According to Jewish burial customs" is too free; a word-for-word translation of the Greek text gives us, "as is the custom of the Jews in laying out a body." *Entaphia-zo,* the Greek verb used, can only mean "lay out"; if "bury" had been intended, then the proper verb would have been *thapto.* Thus John does not specifically say that all the requirements for laying out a body were complied with, much less that a definitive burial took place.

The verb translated "to wrap" (*deo*) means "to tie, to bind." It cannot really apply to the swathing with small strips of cloth as suggested by The New English Bible. It cannot apply at all to wrapping in a large, single sheet. There is, however, a variant reading of some authority in the early Greek manuscripts that is supported by early Syriac translations. The verb used in these is *enilesan* (from *eneileo*), the same verb that Mark uses to describe the wrapping of the body in the sheet. It is a much more appropriate verb for the application of either a sheet or strips of cloth, so it is quite difficult to understand why a copyist would replace it with the problematic *deo.*

As to the "strips of linen cloth," *othonia,* in which, John says, the body was wrapped, *othonion* means much the same as *sindon*—a piece of linen in any of its applications. In the plural, as used by John, it can only designate a plurality of linen cloths. How, then, can this be reconciled with the single sheet referred to in the Synoptics or with the Shroud of Turin? There are several theories:

1. The sheet mentioned by the Synoptics was, there and then, torn into strips, thus becoming the "cloths" observed by John. This solution, said to go back to Salmasius, does reconcile with the Synoptics, if we can accept it; but it is also fatal to the

authenticity of the Shroud, and there is absolutely
no evidence to support the assumption that bands
or bandages swathed the corpses of Jews, either as
a general custom or in special situations.

2. *Othonia* means a variety of cloths, not many
cloths of the same size and shape. This, too, is an
old solution, recently revived with fresh force by A.
Vaccari, a Shroud scholar, who points to a papyrus
inventory of the personal effects of an agent of the
Roman government who made a trip from upper
Egypt to Antioch in about A.D. 320. In the listing,
under the general heading *"Othonia"* are grouped a
variety of linens, including four *sindone*s and two
kinds of handkerchiefs (*fakeria*). If we accept this
theory, then John's references to the *othonia* could
designate the large sheet of linen singled out by the
Synoptics plus the handkerchief that was used to
cover the face (if that is the meaning of the phrase
to be discussed below), and perhaps smaller cloths
used to tie the jaw, hands and feet.

This theory is more acceptable than the first,
since it is entirely feasible that such a variety of
cloths was used in the disposition of Jesus' body.
The verb *deo* still poses a problem, for while it
would be appropriate in referring to the binding of
the hands, feet and jaw, it is still incorrect as it
applies to the application of the *sindon,* for which
the textual variant *eneileo* ("wrap") is better.

3. According to the last theory, *othonia* does
mean linen bands, but refers only to those that
were used to secure the hands, feet and jaw. In *The
Shroud of Turin,* Professor Werner Bulst, former
professor of fundamental theology in the Jesuit
theological seminary at Frankfurt am Main, claims
a measure of originality for this idea, which alone
explains the use of the verb *deo.* That such methods
of binding might have been applied in the case of
Jesus is reasonable to assume. The binding of a

deceased's jaw is common even today. The tying of
the hands and the feet was a practicality, necessary
to counteract the forces of rigor mortis and make it
easier to transport the body to and into the tomb.
In addition, such bindings would allow a more
dignified way of laying out the body.

Bulst's theory is fine as far as it goes, but he fails
to explain why John would only mention the insig-
nificant bindings and disregard the *sindon* itself. To
take it to its end, we must understand that John
was writing for Greek, non-Jewish readers. For
their benefit, he might well have thought it necessary to explain that the bands and especially the
spices were traditional appurtenances of Jewish
burial. He said nothing of the *sindon* because it, or
at least the way it was draped over Jesus, had
nothing to do with traditional Jewish burial customs.

Moving forward in John's text, on Sunday morning Mary of Magdala made her way to the tomb
for an unspecified purpose. Seeing that the stone
had been removed, she ran to tell Peter that the
body had been stolen. Peter and another disciple
(John himself, it is widely believed) ran to the tomb.
John arrived first and stopped at the door. He saw
the *othonia* "lying there." Peter then entered the
tomb and saw not merely the *othonia,* but also "the
*sudarium* which had been over Jesus' head, not
lying with the *othonia* but folded by itself in place.
[In some editions of the Bible, Peter's discovery of
the linen cloths is also mentioned in Luke (24:12),
but most contemporary scholars believe the passage
to be an interpolation from John.] Then the disciple
who had reached the tomb first went in too; and he
saw and believed. Until then they had not understood

the Scriptures, which showed that he must rise from the dead" (John 20:1–9).

The *sudarium* is a new term, a new piece of cloth not mentioned before. It means handkerchief or napkin (literally "sweat cloth"), and no other meaning is attributed in either Greek or Latin, from which the Greeks took the word. Accepting the first explanation of *othonia* cited above, the sudarium is a cloth that enfolded the head while the rest of the body was bandaged like a mummy, the most unlikely of possibilities. Using the second explanation, the sudarium was one of the cloths previously included among the *othonia*, now singled out for special mention. By the third theory, the sudarium could be anything other than the cloths used for binding the hands, feet and jaw.

It is not fatal to the authenticity of the Shroud if, in addition to the actual burial cloth (*sindon*), some other cloths were also used in the burial of Jesus: the *othonia* for binding the hands, feet and jaw; and the sudarium for covering the face. Such bindings and face cloths were in common use at the time, and according to several medical authorities, the face cloth would probably have been an extremely thin and porous veil which would not have hindered the transmission of the images to the Shroud. The cloth wrapped over the head and tied under the jaw to keep the mouth closed in death would have been heavier and thicker, and thus its use could explain the reason that no image appears on the Shroud where the crown of the head would have been positioned against it.

It is thus possible, though problematic, to explain the cloths John saw applied to Jesus' body, and later in the tomb, without denying authenticity to the

Shroud. Yet, although numerous scholars and exegetes have tried, there is just no way that the discrepancies and problems introduced by John's choice of wordage (or the corruption thereof by copyists of the original and subsequent texts) can be completely resolved on the basis of existing documents. But as perplexing as these problems are, they are essentially issues of a linguistic rather than an archaeological bent. And in light of the medical evidence for the Shroud's authenticity, they seem minor indeed.

In no other way does the Shroud or its markings conflict with the Gospels, with other historical sources, or with our present archaeological knowledge.

# IV

## *The Lost Millennium*

In historical terms, the Shroud of Turin can be
traced back with certainty to 1356, but its appearance in Lirey, France, in that year remains unex-
plained. Its owners deliberately obfuscated the question of its origin, and its exposition gave rise to
accusations and scandals which provide the
substance of the principal arguments of opponents
of the Shroud's authenticity. Another focal argument
against it is the striking lack of references to the relic
from the time of Christ and the Gospels until 1356.
Only one text that refers to the year 1204 mentions
a shroud possessing the unique qualities of the
Shroud of Turin. Overzealous proponents of the
Shroud's legitimacy have, to be sure, adduced many
other texts, but these have served only to fire the
incredulity of those capable of understanding their
wording and context.

The astonishing historical silence which surrounds
the Shroud begins with the Gospels themselves, for
only John refers to the finding of cloths in the tomb,
and he says nothing of the most striking feature of
the Shroud of Turin, namely, the images of the
body. Nonetheless, the burial cloth of Christ certainly occupied the imagination of early Christians. It is
often mentioned in the apocryphal Gospels, and in

one of them, the Gospel According to the Hebrews, it is mentioned that after the resurrection, Jesus gave the Shroud "to the servant of the priest," or "to Simon Peter," the latter being the interpretation of some scholars who believe the text is corrupt. This Gospel, preserved only in fragments, enjoyed the esteem of the fathers of the church, many of whom thought it to be the original version of The Gospel of Matthew.

Early Christian apologists pointed to the finding of the cloths in the tomb as proof of the resurrection. If the body had been stolen, they asked, would it not have been easier to carry it in its shroud? There is no indication, however, that these writers knew any more about the Shroud than what they had read in the Gospels. Another early school of thought within the church held that the cloth spread over the altar for the sacrament of Holy Communion was the symbol of the Shroud.

Saint Nino, who brought Christianity to Georgia during the reign of Constantine the Great (A.D. 274–337), is said to have meditated much on the Shroud as a girl in Jerusalem. When she asked her teacher, Niaphori, "the most learned Christian in Jerusalem," about it, she was told that nothing was known, but that tradition affirmed it had been kept by Saint Peter.

Also during the time of Constantine, Eusebius of Caesarea, sometimes known as the father of ecclesiastical history, wrote to Constantia, the emperor's sister, that a portrait of Christ was an impossibility, since only God knew his spiritual nature, while his physical appearance was forever lost. Eusebius frowned on all pictures and statues which purported to show the actual likeness of Jesus, for such representations were the objects of excessive veneration and, to him, smacked of heathen practices. Still later, Saint Augustine wrote that the representations of Christ were innumerable, "although his appearance, whatever it was, can only have been one."

The first mention of an actual, existent Shroud appears in an account of the Holy Land written in about 570 by a pilgrim from Piacenza. The anonymous chronicler, who lent a ready ear to the tall tales of guides and solemnly reproduced them in his work, reports that the Shroud was said to be preserved in a cave convent by the Jordan. He himself had not seen it, however.

About a century later, Arculph, a French bishop, made a pilgrimage to the Holy Land. On the return voyage, bad weather forced him to put in at Iona, off the coast of Scotland, where the details of his eventful journey were recorded by the Benedictine abbot Adamnan. Among the marvels of Jerusalem was "the shroud which covered Jesus' head in the tomb." It was exposed for veneration every other day, and Arculph saw, venerated and kissed it.

A legend attached to the object on display in Jerusalem, also duly reported, said that it had been stolen after the resurrection by a converted Jew, and that its possession enriched him vastly. When he lay dying, he offered his two sons the choice between all his worldly possessions and the Shroud. The son who chose the possessions promptly squandered them; the one who chose the Shroud was soon as wealthy as his father had been. The Shroud remained in the same family down to the fifth generation, but then it fell into the hands of infidel Jews, who also grew rich from their possession of it. The existence and properties of the Shroud became common knowledge in Jerusalem, and the Christians grew vociferous in claiming it for themselves. The dispute was submitted for judgment to an Arab ruler, who took the Shroud and placed it, with his own hands, in a burning fire. The cloth was not damaged and, before long, it rose from the fire, hovered in the air, and finally fell to earth near the Christian spectators. The Christians glorified God and placed the relic in a church.

Arculph described the Shroud he saw as being about eight feet long, and mentioned neither bloodstains nor images. But if the cloth he saw was the Shroud of Turin, he could hardly have avoided seeing them; and any rationalizations to the contrary are just not acceptable. Nonetheless, Arculph's account has been discussed in almost every study of the Shroud, and some sindonologists have taken great pains to explain away the problematic eight feet; one school believing that the Shroud was folded for display, another that Arculph did indeed see the entire length, but referred to it in terms of the ancient Piedmont foot. The latter, translated into contemporary measurement, would make the shroud Arculph saw equal 13.482 feet, not significantly less than the 14 feet, 3 inches of the Shroud of Turin, and Arculph did qualify his measurement with "about."

All of this is at best an example of the academic pettifoggery that has impaired serious consideration of the Shroud since its discovery. Arculph's account, as well as a number of others which will not be repeated here, proves only one thing: The burial cloth of Christ—existent or not, witnessed or not, one and the same as the Shroud of Turin or not—was felt to be an important symbol of the Christian faith, as were any number of other relics, real or simulated. It should be noted here that in medieval Europe there are known to have been at least forty-three "True Shrouds," both plain and figured, some of these obvious copies of the Shroud of Turin. As only one example of the extreme naïveté with which they were accepted, the famous Shroud of Cadouin was discovered—in 1935—to be a Moslem cloth embroidered with texts praising Allah. Thus all of these ancient, uncorroborated testaments to the existence of the Shroud must be treated with the utmost skepticism.

From about the year 1000 onward, a shroud is mentioned in catalogues of the relics preserved at the imperial court in Constantinople. Again, nothing is said of marks or stains, let alone a discernible image. In 1201 Nicholas Mesarites, patriarch of Constantinople and head of the Eastern church, examined and described those precious relics. The funeral cloths of Christ, he says, "are of linen, of cheap material, such as was available. They still smell of perfume; they have defied decay because they enveloped the ineffable, naked, myrrh-covered corpse after the Passion." If Mesarites saw images, he did not mention them, but some scholars have deduced from his citing of the "naked" body that he knew more than he told, since the concept of a naked Christ, in any circumstances, has not been favorably looked upon throughout the history of Christianity, but is immediately evident on the Shroud.

Finally, in 1204 Robert de Clari, a chronicler of the Fourth Crusade, wrote that before the fall of Constantinople to the Crusaders, a shroud was exhibited every Friday at the church of Saint Mary of the Blachernae, and that on this shroud the figure of Christ was clearly visible. "After the city was taken," he added, "no one, neither Greek nor Frenchman, ever knew what became of it." Since de Clari himself arrived with the Crusaders, however, it would seem that he did not see the relic with his own eyes.

Relics did count as important booty in the sack of Constantinople. Large numbers of venerable objects were sent to Europe, and it was not long before more relics than Constantinople ever had were in circulation there. Cloths advertised as parts of the Holy Shroud found their way almost at once to towns in France and Germany. One "part" remained in Constantinople only to be presented in 1247, along with other relics, to Louis IX of France. Parts of that part were in turn exchanged by the king for other relics. Whatever the fragments of cloth were, they were not from the Shroud of Turin, since, with the exception of those segments destroyed by fire, the Shroud itself is intact.

It is possible that the object described by Robert de Clari was the Shroud of Turin, but if so, no light has ever been shed upon the 152 years that elapsed between its disappearance from Constantinople and its appearance at Lirey.

The documented historical case for the authenticity of the Shroud is thus exceptionally poor and only slightly improved by attempts to explain the silence of historical sources.

To the Jews, it has been argued, anything that touched a corpse was impure; to the Gentiles, crucifixion was the most ignominious of punishments,

and it was unthinkable that a god in human form—
a familiar idea in the Greco-Roman world—would
submit to it. The Shroud had touched what was, at
one point, a corpse, and bore witness in a chillingly
graphic way to the horrors of crucifixion. Under
these circumstances, the custodians of the Shroud,
whoever they were, could not have been eager to
display such a controversial artifact.

The idea of Jesus crucified was so repellent to
early Christians that it significantly affected not only
the spread of the new religion, but also the artistic
tradition that arose from it. There was almost a tacit
law that forbade pictorial representations of the
crucifixion, and this would have imposed even
greater restraint on public expositions and general
knowledge of the Shroud, so stark was the reality of
its depiction.

The earliest pictures of Jesus show him as a
clean-shaven youth. He appears as a fisherman, a
shepherd, a teacher, as the leader of a dance, but
not in any of the degrading phases of the Passion.
The cross became, almost at once, the symbol of the
new religion; but the earliest artistic representations
of the crucifixion date only from the fifth century.
One of these crucifixion scenes, on a wooden panel
of the door of Santa Sabina in Rome, is also one of
the earliest works of art in which Jesus is shown
bearded. Crucifixion scenes became a little more
common in the sixth and seventh centuries, but as
late as 692, an ecclesiastical council at Constantinople found it necessary to ordain that the figure of
Christ be depicted on the cross, and not merely
symbolized by a star or a lamb.

The politics of the church continued to be of a
kind that might have discouraged any emphasis on

the Shroud. In 725, a tendency of eastern Christianity came strongly to the fore: the use of icons or devotional images was condemned, and the imperial dynasty led the struggle to suppress such pictures and relics. The controversy lasted, with interruptions, until 845. The Iconoclasts, or opponents of the images, would have had little use for the Shroud, but the iconodules, or picture-venerators, would have had every reason to preserve it, perhaps in hiding. If the iconodules did know of the Shroud, however, there are no references to it, and it is astonishing that they would make no mention of it in their polemical writings, particularly in light of their citing of another image of Christ's face on a cloth as a sign of divine approval of these images. And after the final defeat of iconoclasm in 845, there can have been no reason to conceal the existence of the Shroud and every reason to see that it received the widest possible display. But again we are faced with silence.

Thus, with the exception of Robert de Clari's all-too-vague account of the disappearance of a figured shroud from Constantinople in 1204, if the Shroud of Turin did exist before 1356, there are no reliable reports to justify such a claim. Certainly none of the references to Holy Shrouds or burial cloths can be said to designate anything with the unusual properties of the Shroud as we know it. This disconcerting lack of pedigree has given much ammunition to the critics on historical grounds, and at the same time has moved some proponents into almost absurd rationalizations for the millennium's silence.

Now we must ask, is it possible the Shroud did exist, was known, does have a somewhat documented history, but was thought to be something entirely different from what it is? It is with these questions in mind that we must confront the Holy Image of Edessa.

# V

## *The Holy Image of Edessa*

Edessa was a Syrian border town and early center of Christianity, which was probably introduced there sometime during the second century A.D. During the Persian siege of that city in 544, a cloth was found inside a wall over the city gate. On it there existed what was believed to be a miraculous image of Christ. This cloth, generally referred to as the Holy Image of Edessa or the Edessan Image, is the most important of several such pictures or images of Christ which began to turn up in the sixth century and were said to be *acheiropoieton*—"not made with hands."

In searching for a history of the Shroud in the millennium following the crucifixion, we find little of significance except this mysterious Edessan Image. Could it be possible, then, that these two images of Christ are intrinsically related?

If authentic, the Shroud of Turin has its origin at the crucifixion. Other than its remarkable discovery in the wall in 544, the origin of the Edessan Image is unknown. There is, of course, the standard and seemingly obligatory progression of legends. According to Eusebius, who based his tale on documents he claimed existed in the Edessan archives, Abgar V, king of Edessa from A.D. 13 to 50, was ill and became interested in new religions. Thus he sent an envoy to Jesus, asking him to visit his court. Jesus declined, but sent a letter promising good things for Abgar and his people. Eusebius mentions no image in his account, but given his animosity toward depictions of Christ generally, such an omission would not have been out of character. According to the fourth-century *Doctrine of Addai,* however, Abgar's envoy, Ananias, painted a portrait of Jesus. Still later, in about 730, John Damascene wrote that the accepted origin of the Edessan Image was that Ananias was not able to paint a satisfactory portrait, and so Jesus obligingly picked up the cloth and pressed it to his face, thereby imprinting it with a miraculous likeness of himself.

Having virtually no factual substance, these stories seem nothing more than attempts, undoubtedly successful at the time, at providing an acceptable provenance for the perplexing cloth that most certainly did exist, and which, in the words of the Reverend Maurus Green, a British priest and historian, "acquired an artistic, theological and political importance far greater than any other icon before or since."

During the siege of Edessa by the Persians in 544, the newly found Image was paraded around the barricaded city, miraculously aiding in the repulsion of the attackers, or so it was believed.

By the time of the Iconoclast controversy (725–845), Edessa was no longer part of the Byzantine Empire, and the Image was thus safe from the fury of the Iconoclasts. It was not safe, however, from the Byzantines. Father Green writes:

Once Iconoclasm was finally defeated in 845, Orthodox Constantinople could not long remain without possession of its most powerful weapon. In 943, the old emperor, Romanus Lecapenus, sent his army to invade Syria with special instructions to obtain the Image. Edessa was besieged. The city would be spared, if the Image was handed over in exchange for two hundred Moslem hostages. After long negotiations and unsuccessful attempts by the citizens to pass off two copies as the real thing, the Byzantine army returned in triumph in 944. The Image, by now known as the *Mandylion,* was given the welcome reserved to conquering generals. It was taken with great piety round the city walls, in through the Golden Gates to Santa Sophia, to be lodged finally in the imperial Chapel of the Bucoleon. Christ himself had entered his own city. Henceforth he would guard it against all attacks, as he had once guarded Edessa. On occasion his Image was carried round the walls as a defense measure, when the city was under siege.

Until the Crusaders ravaged the city in 1204, the Edessan Image ranked as the most treasured relic of the capital; after that date its fate is unclear. And after that same date, the figured cloth referred to by Robert de Clari as the Shroud also disappeared . . . from the same city, possibly from the same resting place. Were the two actually only one? And was the Edessan Image what we now know as the Shroud of Turin?

British historian Ian Wilson, who has spent years studying this aspect of the Shroud's existence, believes it is. He commissioned the first complete translation of *De Imagine Edessena,* an "official" history of the Edessan Image written by a member of the court of the tenth-century emperor Constantine Porphyrogenitus. In that history is a description of how the Image appeared to the Byzantines: ". . . a moist secretion, without any coloring or artificial aid." A rather strange description of anything that might be considered a painted icon. But an almost perfect description of the image visible on the Shroud of Turin.

One of the problems Wilson faces in linking the Edessan Image with the Shroud of Turin is that the dominant tradition of the Edessan Image maintains that only a face is visible and not the entire body. Wilson contends, however, that he has found evidence to support the thesis that whenever the Edessan Image was shown, it was "doubled in four." And folding the Shroud of Turin in exactly that way will produce the same "disembodied" head seen on copies of the Edessan Image. Additional evidence in support of this contention are the two groups of small, dark circles visible especially at the level of the loins on the dorsal image of the Shroud. As was mentioned earlier, the generally accepted notion is that these were caused by some fire prior to the one that damaged the Shroud in Chambéry, but Wilson believes the marks were made by whatever naillike devices were used to keep the long cloth in its folded position.

Since Ian Wilson is presently preparing his own manuscript on the Shroud for publication, it would be somewhat unfair to reveal any more of his research or thesis. There is, however, one other area of study which offers some support for the belief that the Edessan Image and the Shroud of Turin are one and the same. That area involves the many artistic reproductions of Christ's face that began to appear in the sixth century, and is referred to by sindonologists as the iconographic theory.

Certainly Jesus had been depicted before that time, but it is during the sixth century that the traditional appearance of Christ—with a long, oval face, shoulder-length hair, mustache and a beard (usually forked), long nose, deep-set eyes and a pronounced arched eyebrow—became the dominant artistic conception. And these features are not inconsistent with those that can be discerned on the Shroud. Is it possible, then, that the Shroud served as the model for these depictions, but, for whatever reasons, was at the time known as the Edessan Image?

To put this iconographic argument into context, and to explain an extremely complex set of premises as simply as possible, let us construct a speculative history of the Shroud/Image from the crucifixion until its disappearance from Constantinople in 1204.

Following the crucifixion and resurrection, Simon Peter or some other disciple came into possession of the Shroud. If the images were then visible, he was aware that he held the most miraculous of all miracles—a self-portrait of the risen Savior. Even if the images had not yet formed on the linen (a theory ventured by some students of the Shroud), the cloth itself would have been deemed valuable, if only as a personal keepsake of the disciple. But in either case, the cloth was also bloody and had touched the corpse of a crucified man. Neither Jew nor Gentile, no matter how strong his dedication to Jesus, would have felt comfortable in its possession. In addition, while such a graphic reminder of Jesus' sacrifice might indeed have served as a powerful symbol of the burgeoning new religion, it would just as certainly have been sought out by its opponents and destroyed.

Its owner, perceiving all this, carefully hid it away, either hoping to reclaim it himself in more propitious times, or, in effect, willing it to future Christians. After hiding it, he may have mentioned it to other early Christians from time to time, thus adding some substance, albeit unverifiable, to the rumors and legends about its existence.

Its hiding place, the brick city wall of Edessa, was discovered in 544, and while its new owners did not know—or did not want others to know—exactly what it was, they did identify it as a miraculous portrait of Jesus. But this was a portrait of a naked, crucified, suffering Christ, and both the artistic conventions and general concept of Christ during this time studiously avoided such portrayals.

As the Reverend Edward A. Wuenschel has written:

> Even after Constantine abolished crucifixion, and the cross was brought into the open as an honored symbol, it took about three centuries for Christian artists to abandon their reverential reticence, but it was Christ living and triumphant, clad in a robe of glory and wearing a royal crown, that they portrayed on the cross, not Christ in agony or in death. It was only in the eleventh century that they ventured to be more realistic. The complete realism of the crucifix which is so familiar to us now did not make its appearance till the thirteenth century, and it was developed principally in the West.
>
> Now on the Shroud the effects of Christ's crucifixion are visible in all their stark reality, more

vivid and more appalling than in any artistic work. And not only the crucifixion. There are also the marks of all the other humiliating tortures of the Passion and traces of the process which took place after death. It is reasonable, therefore, to suppose that the Shroud was kept more or less hidden for centuries and a prudent silence observed about the imprint. . . . Those who imagine that the guardians of the Shroud should have gone about waving it like a banner show little understanding of the condition of the Christian Orient.

So the real Shroud/Image was kept discreetly out of sight. The few priests and members of royalty who did view it saw a cloth that was folded and pinned in such a way that the battered and bleeding body was kept hidden and only the remarkable majesty of the face revealed.

At the time the Shroud/Image was discovered, the church was combatting the heresy of the Monophysites, who denied the human nature of Christ. The evidence of the Shroud itself would have provided a clear illustration of that human nature, but since it was considered too graphic to be shown, a competent copy, supported by the Edessan legend of its miraculous origin, was probably deemed sufficient to rout the heretics. The fifth and sixth centuries were not sophisticated times, and just about any religious argument buttressed with enough authority could have been put over and enforced.

Thus did an artist copy the facial image, adhering to the details of Christ's countenance as witnessed on the cloth, but changing the misty negative image of the death mask into a more conventionally acceptable portrait of the living Christ. The newly painted "Edessan Image"—the public accepting the copy as the real thing—met with great success, and soon the popular demand for more copies representing the "true likeness" of Christ was such that other selected artists were allowed or encouraged to make duplications. Whether they worked from the actual Shroud or from the copy, these artists were scrupulous in their attention to detail, and even though the haziness of the Shroud's image must have made it exceptionally difficult to copy, the similarities between it and a number of the reproductions are striking.

The Iconoclast controversy that raged from 725 to 845 gave additional reasons to keep the Shroud hidden and well protected, and even afterward, it is unlikely that many people were allowed to see it.

When the Byzantine army came to appropriate the Shroud/Image in 943, the Edessans tried several times to pass off some of their better copies as the real thing. But the Byzantines knew exactly what they were after, and the Shroud/Image that entered Constantinople in 944 was undoubtedly the original. It remained there until the sack of the city by members of the Fourth Crusade in 1204. During their plunder, the Crusaders took everything they could lay their hands on, and what they couldn't carry back to the West, they destroyed. Among the spoils was the Holy Shroud.

Now this history is nothing but speculation. It takes into account the known currents of the church, particularly as they affected attitudes toward the visual display of Christ's likeness; it expands upon the few facts that are known; and it depends heavily on the similarities between the artistic depictions of Christ that began to appear in the sixth century and the facial image that is evident on the Shroud of

Turin. The most prominent of these artistic reproductions are those of the *mandylion* class, which were painted on cloth and almost certainly had their inspiration in the Edessan Image, whatever it really was.

This speculative account does make sense if the Shroud is authentic. If it could be proven, it would provide the Shroud with the continuous historical thread it so vitally needs. But it is open to challenge on a number of points. Sophisticated historians and art authorities can introduce contradictions and inconsistencies, but both supporters and opponents are dealing with fragments of knowledge, and in the end—unless Ian Wilson or others are able to add significantly to the facts of this period—it is unlikely that any concrete and completely acceptable history of the Shroud will be determined.

# VI

## The Pilgrimage of the Shroud

If the Shroud of Turin has only a speculative history before 1356, it has an exceptionally stormy one thereafter. Sometime between 1353 and 1356, the Shroud mysteriously turned up in the possession of Geoffroy de Charny (*père*) in Lirey, France. The exact date cannot be pinpointed, but since de Charny died in 1356, that is the earliest date we can use with certainty.

Little is known of Geoffroy de Charny; nothing is known of how he acquired this mysterious possession. A rather prominent French knight of the period, the lord of the district of Lirey, he is first heard of in 1337, when he served under the Count of Eu in the wars of Guyenne and Languedoc. In 1345, he accompanied Humbert II, dauphin of Viennois, on a foray into infidel territory. In 1348, in an attempt to take Calais from the English by ruse, he was captured by the British, from whose clutches he was ransomed by the king of France for 1,000 gold écus. In 1355, he was designated to carry the battle standard of the king, a signal honor. An authority on questions of chivalry, he wrote a book on the subject, and was the author as well of verses expressing a rather stern sense of morality.

A series of documents dated from 1343 to 1356

indicate de Charny's sponsorship of a church at Lirey, in the diocese of Troyes. The documents show that Philip VI (king of France, 1328-1350) amortized income for the pious foundation; that two popes—Clement VI and Innocent VI—approved the regulations of the new canonry and enriched it with indulgences; and that the bishop of Troyes, Henri de Poitiers, gave the undertaking his blessing.

In the past, some scholars have asserted that de Charny founded the church for the specific purpose of housing and displaying the "true Burial Sheet of Christ." There are absolutely no documents to support such an assertion, and the details of the documents that do exist concerning the foundation of the church—none of which mentions the Shroud in any context—tend to further refute the claim.

The evidence that the Shroud was displayed at Lirey during the life of de Charny is based on two documents. The first is a letter written by Pierre d'Arcis, de Poitiers' successor as bishop of Troyes, dated 1389. The letter states that the Shroud had been exposed at Lirey thirty-four years previously, "or thereabouts," or about 1355. The second document, a decree issued by (anti-)Pope Clement VII in 1390, mentions that the Shroud was "reverently placed" at Lirey by de Charny.

De Charny never divulged how, where or from whom he had obtained the Shroud, and took his important secret to the grave. If, however, the Shroud had indeed been at Constantinople before its fall, at least a kernel of speculation is possible. According to the Reverend A. J. Otterbein in his *New Catholic Encyclopedia* article, "It was not likely that [the Shroud] was taken to France at the time when the fall of Constantinople to the Orientals was foreseen. Further, it is known that the Latin Emperor's prime minister, who had access to [the Shroud], returned to the West shortly before the fall of Constantinople. He was of the family of the wife of Geoffroy de Charny. . . ."

As likely as this hypothesis might seem, it still leaves the question of who had the Shroud from 1204 until 1353–1356. Another unsupported theory suggests that the Shroud was given to de Charny by King Philip VI. In either case, the question remains: If de Charny had the Shroud in his possession for any period of time before his death, why is the relic not mentioned in any of the documents or records of the church at Lirey?

Nothing more is heard of the Shroud until 1389. In that year, Geoffroy de Charny (*fils*) obtained from Pierre de Thury, cardinal of Saint Susan and legate of the pope to Charles VI (king of France, 1380–1422), permission to exhibit the Shroud at Lirey. In his decree of 1390, Clement VII refers to this as permission to exhibit "a semblance or representation of the sudarium of our Lord." Letters from Charles VI confirmed the permission.

No permission was sought from Pierre d'Arcis, then bishop of Troyes. It was not long, however, before the extravagant ceremonies which attended the Shroud at Lirey, and the vast crowds of pilgrims attracted by the miraculous relic, drew d'Arcis' attention and his wrath. Angered by the slight to his authority and by the number of pilgrims deserting Troyes in favor of the more sensational attraction of Lirey, d'Arcis convened a synod (an ecclesiastical council), at which he forbade the clergy of the diocese to speak of the Shroud, whether for good or evil. He rebuked the dean of Lirey for exceeding the authorization of the cardinal-legate, which permitted modest expositions only, and forbade him on pain of excommunication to show the Shroud in any way to anyone at all.

The clergy of Lirey retorted by appealing to the Holy See. While waiting for a reply, they continued to expose the Shroud with the utmost ceremoniousness and solemnity. The messenger dispatched by the canons to the papal court at Avignon returned with a document from Clement VII in which the permission issued by the cardinal-legate was confirmed. The pope, moreover, imposed "eternal silence" regarding the subject of the Holy Shroud on Pierre d'Arcis.

The bishop, far from falling or remaining silent, immediately complained to Charles VI, and on August 4, 1389, the king withdrew the permission to expose the Shroud that he had previously granted. Furthermore, Charles wrote to the bailiff of Troyes, Jean de Venderesse, instructing him to confiscate the Shroud in the name of the crown. The bailiff's visit to Lirey is commemorated in a memorandum drawn up and signed by him on August 15; a second memorandum of the same date includes details that had "unfortunately" been omitted from the first. At Lirey, the good bailiff was met with a bewildering mass of sophisms, with appeals to the authority of Geoffroy de Charny and of Clement VII, and finally with a flat refusal to surrender the Shroud.

Baffled by the obstinacy of the canons, and himself unwilling to give up the fight, Pierre d'Arcis then composed and addressed to Clement VII the long letter which later critics of the Shroud seized upon as the principal historical justification for rejecting its authenticity.

The basic substance of the letter (which will be reproduced in the following chapter) follows: According to d'Arcis, the first exposition of the Shroud (which he describes as being in 1355, "or thereabouts") was undertaken without the authorization of the then bishop of Troyes, Henri de Poitiers. Henri proceeded to conduct an investigation. A committee of theologians and other prudent men assured him that the Shroud at Lirey could not possibly be genuine, since the Gospels say nothing of any imprints on the shroud found in the tomb. Further inquiries made by Henri showed that the Shroud possessed by the canons of Lirey was a forgery, and this finding was corroborated by "the artist who had painted it": to wit, that it was "the work of human skill and not miraculously wrought or bestowed." (We will deal fully with the implications of this charge later, but suffice it to say for now that no documents of the alleged de Poiters investigation survive, and if they did at the time, d'Arcis neither introduced nor even mentioned them.)

Pierre d'Arcis' letter went on to condemn in the roundest terms the avarice and cupidity of the canons of Lirey, which led them to: expose the Shroud with greater ceremony than attended the Holy Eucharist; put into circulation rumors that it was the True Shroud and that it performed miracles; and encourage among the faithful the notion that its authenticity was sanctioned by the Holy See. D'Arcis voiced his concern for the souls of the faithful and expressed his confidence that permission to expose it had been obtained from the legate and the pope only by serious misrepresentations. He regarded himself as justified in ignoring the pope's injunction to eternal silence.

What d'Arcis' letter lacked in proof and substance, it amply made up in rhetoric; and it must have been persuasive. But neither had Geoffroy (*fils*) been idle. He had addressed to the pope a complaint against the measures taken by the bishop, the king and the bailiff.

On January 6, 1390, Clement VII, assailed on all sides by appeals, complaints and recriminations, issued no fewer than three bulls on the subject of the Shroud:

1. A general decree *ad futuram rei memoriam:* The exposition of the relic is permitted, but the ceremonies censured by the bishop are forbidden. The relic is to be shown in a discreet way, and during the exposition it must be proclaimed loudly and intelligibly that "it is not the True Shroud of Our Lord, but a painting or picture made in the semblance or representation of the shroud."

2. To Pierre d'Arcis: He is forbidden to oppose the exposition of the relic, provided that the exposition take place in the manner and under the conditions prescribed by the pope.

3. To the ecclesiastical judges of Langres, Autun and Châlons-sur-Marne: They are exhorted to make known to all, and to assure the implementation of, the dispositions of the pope with regard to the Shroud.

It is presumed that the pope's directives were carried out for some years without incident, for nothing more is heard of the Shroud until 1418. In that year, Humbert, Count de la Roche, issued a receipt to the canons of Lirey for the relics and church ornaments confided to his care for the duration of a period of war and unrest. Humbert had married Marguerite, the daughter of Geoffroy de Charny (*fils*) and thereby became lord of Lirey. He died without returning the relics that had been placed in his care, among which treasures was what was dutifully recorded as "the semblance or representation of the shroud of Our Lord."

When the canons of Lirey tried to recover their possessions from the widow Marguerite, they found it necessary to summon her before the judicial court of Dôle. On May 8, 1443, she was compelled by threat of endless legal complications to surrender to the canons the "several relics and ornaments" that had been entrusted to her husband. But the area of Lirey was, in Marguerite's opinion, still unsafe; and she was also quick to point out that she was not bound by the signature of her husband with regard to the Shroud, which she claimed had been taken in war by her grandfather and could therefore be regarded as her own property. She did, however, promise to return the Shroud after three years, and agreed to pay compensation—twelve francs per annum—for the resulting loss of alms to the canons.

Three years later, the canons summoned Marguerite before the ecclesiastical judge of Besançon. She appeared on July 18, 1447, only to voice afresh her apprehension at leaving the Shroud in a disturbed area. The canons, with exemplary patience, consented to an additional delay of two years, but raised their demand of yearly compensation to fifteen francs.

In 1449 Marguerite and the Shroud appeared in Hainaut (a medieval county in northern France, now territory divided by Belgium and France). Ac-

cording to the chronicler Zantifliet, she arrived at
Chimay (a town in the Hainaut district) with "a
piece of linen on which was admirably depicted the
form of the body of Our Lord." Rumor proclaimed
this to be the True Shroud of Christ, and the faithful
came streaming from the surrounding provinces to
venerate it. When the matter reached the attention
of Jean de Heinsberg, bishop of Liège, he dispatched
two professors of theology to look into it. In the
course of their investigations they required Marguerite to produce the documents that authorized her to
display the relic. She showed them three bulls of
Clement VII and an authorization issued by Cardinal "Pierre de Luna" (presumably Pierre de
Thury). Each of these documents, according to the
chronicler—and he reproduced textually one of the
Clementine bulls—stated explicitly that the relic in
question was not the True Shroud of Christ.

At the expiration of the second extension that
had been granted Marguerite for the return of the
Shroud (October 28, 1449), she was not to be
found in Burgundy. On November 6, she was represented before the provost of Troyes by her brother, Charles de Noyers. The canons pressed, once
again, for the surrender of their treasure; Charles
recognized their right to it, but again obtained an
extension of three years. He promised, in Marguerite's name, to fortify Lirey, which she still regarded
as an unsafe resting place for the Shroud. Once
more, the payment of an annual sum was arranged,
even though neither of the previous sums had ever
been paid.

Marguerite and the Shroud next appear in Savoy,
at the court of Duke Louis I. On March 22, 1452,
by all accounts, she presented the Shroud to the

duke, who placed it in the sacristy of the Sainte Chapelle at Chambéry, France. No document attests to this transaction; nor is it clarified by references in later documents. Neither is there mention of the Shroud in the document in which Louis enfeoffs to Marguerite the town and manor of Mirabel in 1453, nor in the document in which he presents her with the town and manor of Flumet in 1455, as compensation for Mirabel, which has in the meantime been taken from her.

It was some time before the canons of Lirey recognized the full extent of their misfortune, but when they did, they were no longer content with halfway measures. On May 30, 1457, the ecclesiastical judge of Besançon, after a pro forma exhortation to return the Shroud to its rightful owners, issued against Marguerite a writ of excommunication.

Communication did not lapse, however, between the canons and their patroness. Marguerite promised to pay a compensation of eight hundred gold ducats for the Shroud, and on January 19, 1458, she was summoned before the provost of Troyes to explain her failure to keep that promise. Once more, Charles de Noyers appeared in her place. Once more, promises were made, this time by Charles in his own name. The sum would be paid, and an additional payment of three hundred pounds would reimburse the canons for the expenses of justice. It was also agreed that the relevant papal bulls would be surrendered to the canons, who were anxious to be able to document their ownership of the Shroud. It was agreed that the excommunication of Marguerite would be suspended until the date fixed for

Plate 1

This sixteenth-century painting by the artist Giulio Clovio illustrates the manner in which the Shroud was wrapped lengthwise around the body of Jesus, allowing both the frontal and dorsal images to be reproduced on it. Although cropped in this photo, at the top of the painting are three angels displaying a crude reproduction of the Shroud, complete with its images and the markings left by the Chambéry fire of 1532.

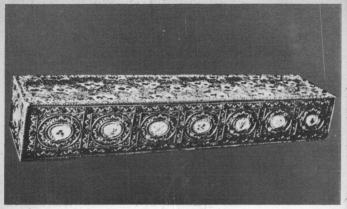

Plate 2

The ornate silver casket in which the Shroud has been kept for centuries.

Plate 3

An enlargement of the cloth from which the Shroud was woven. It is pure linen, a herringbone pattern woven in what is referred to as a three-to-one twill. Material of this type is believed to have been commonly available in Palestine during the time of Jesus.

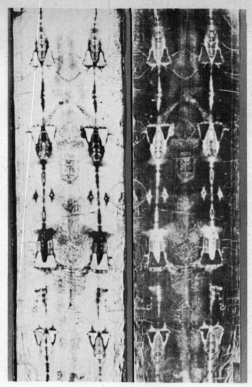

Plate 4 (Left)

The full Shroud as it appears to the naked eye, with the
frontal and dorsal images head to head. The dark lines
which run the entire length of the Shroud, the triangular
patches sewn on by the Poor Clares and the large, lozenge-
shaped stains are the results of the Chambéry fire.


Plate 5 (Right)

The Shroud as it appears on a photographic negative. The
continuous mistlike stains which comprise the body images
have positive (or normal) characteristics of light and shade,
'le the bloodstains have negative characteristics.

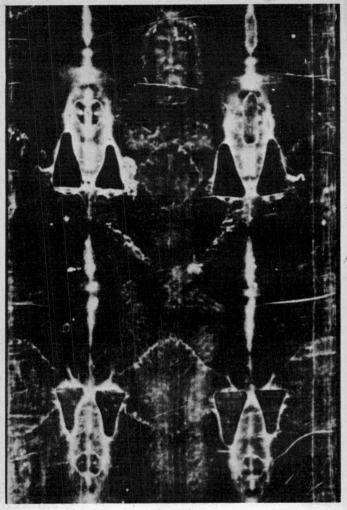

Plate 6

The frontal image as it appears on a photographic negative.

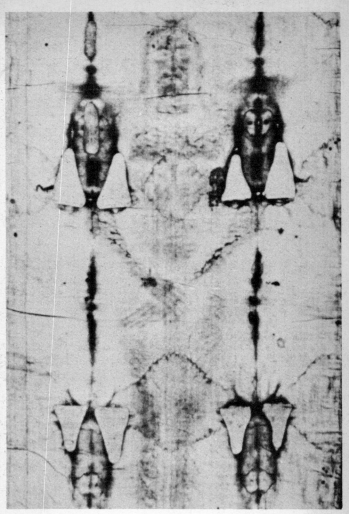

Plate 7

The frontal image as it appears to the naked eye. Since the Shroud is itself a "negative," in the photographic sense, its colors and positions are reversed from the way they appear in reality.

Plate 8

The face of the man on the Shroud, as it is seen on a photographic negative. The trickles of blood in the hair and on
the forehead are results of the crown of thorns. Art experts
have found on the face a number of physical details and
anomalies which are also present on early icons believed to
be copies of the Edessan Image.

Plate 9

The images on the Shroud were used as the model for this sculpture of the crucifixion by Peter Weyland. The crown of thorns is more like a cap than the traditionally accepted circlet. As on the Shroud, the nails are pierced through the wrists rather than the palms; both feet are joined by one nail; and the expanded rib cage and contracted epigastric hollow point to death brought on by hanging from the arms.

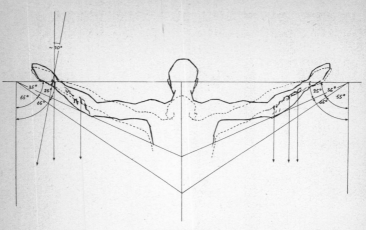

Plate 10

This diagram illustrates Dr. Pierre Barbet's theory that the body of Jesus alternately lifted and sagged on the cross—the reason that the blood evident on the forearms flowed in different directions.

Plate 12—Plate 13 (Right)

These two X-ray-like diagrams show how the nail pierced the wrist of the man on the Shroud, according to Dr. Barbet's calculations.

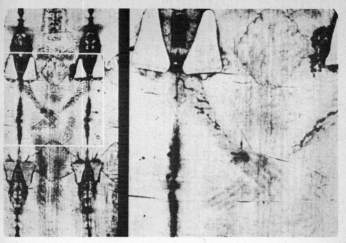

Plate 11

An enlarged detail of the Shroud's frontal image. Note the wound in the wrist, the blood flows on the forearms and the large patch of blood which flowed from the wound in the side. Both thumbs are hidden from view, an anomaly explained by Dr. Barbet's experiments with cadavers.

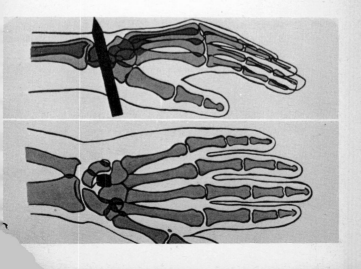

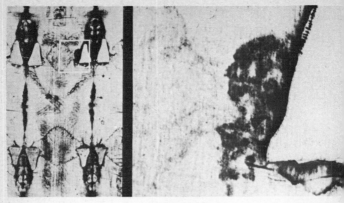

Plate 14

An enlarged detail from the frontal image of the Shroud shows the large patch of blood and serous fluid that flowed from the wound in the side.

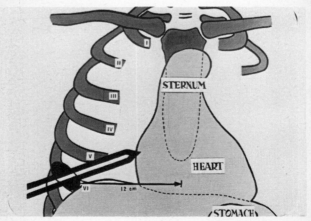

Plate 15

This diagram illustrates Dr. Barbet's theory that the lance entered the body between the fifth and sixth ribs and then pierced the heart.

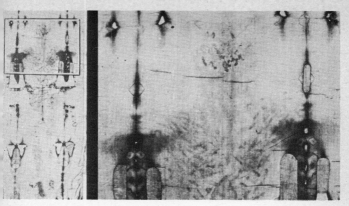

Plate 16

An enlarged detail of the dorsal image shows the number of punctures inflicted by the crown of thorns and the excoriations that resulted from the chafing of the cross and the scourging.

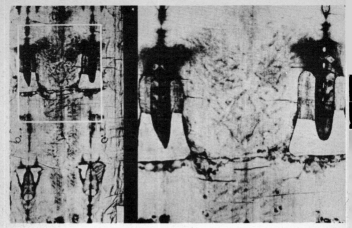

Plate 17

An enlarged detail of the dorsal image shows the many scourge wounds. The transverse flow of blood across the lower back is believed to have issued from the heart when Jesus was being carried to the tomb in a horizontal position.

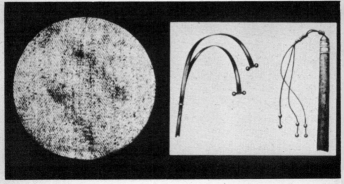

Plate 18

Plate 19

An enlargement of the dumb-bell-shaped wounds inflicted by the *flagrum*.

Reproductions of the Roman *flagrum* used to scourge those marked for execution.

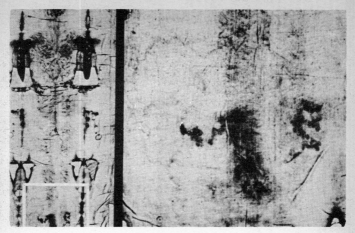

Plate 20

This enlarged detail of the dorsal image shows the somewhat hazy area of the feet. They are turned inward, indicating
that one nail was used to affix both feet to the cross.

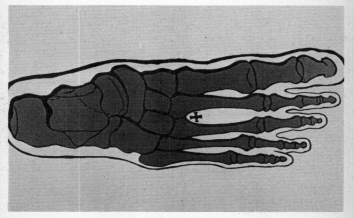

Plate 21

The "X" in this diagram indicates the position of the nail
that joined the feet to the cross.

Plate 22

The Royal Chapel of the Cathedral of Saint John the Baptist
in Turin, Italy. The Shroud has been kept in a vault on the
altar here since 1578.

Plate 23

The Shroud on display inside the Cathedral of Turin during the exposition of 1933.

Plate 24

The Shroud on display outside the Cathedral of Turin during the 1933 exposition.

payment—October 1, 1458—and that upon payment it would lapse altogether.

On October 7 of the following year Marguerite died, having paid not a penny of compensation and still under sentence of excommunication.

The canons, cheated of their due by Marguerite and Charles, next approached the duke of Savoy. In Paris on February 6, 1464, Louis I issued a document in which the history of the Shroud was resumed and the conditions under which Marguerite had "transferred" it to the House of Savoy were left discreetly vague. Recognizing the substantial loss and diminution of income suffered by the canons, the duke assigned to them in perpetuity an annual income of fifty gold francs, demanding in return that a mass be said every year for the Holy Spirit, and after the duke's decease, for the repose of his soul.

In the midst of all this, the canons had not forgotten Marguerite, upon whose memory they heaped reproofs, and from whose agent, Philibert Thibaut, they refused to lift the ban of excommunication. On May 23, 1465, the duke wrote to them from Paris, chiding them for their intransigent attitudes.

A petition of 1472 or 1482—the date is uncertain—was addressed by the canons of Lirey to the king of France. The story of the Shroud is once again related; yet this time the canons complain of the duke of Savoy's failure to honor his financial obligations. In the petition, the canons request that the king himself assign the revenues to them until such time as compensation for the loss of revenue from the Shroud can be obtained. A fragmentary order issued by King Louis XI to the bailiffs of Sens,

Troyes and Chaumont does not make clear the result of the petition.

In 1473, the canons dispatched representatives to Duchess Yolande—regent for Philibert, the grandson of Louis I of Savoy—their purpose to claim eight years of arrears in the income promised them in 1464. The outcome of the embassy is unknown.

It is known, however, that the Shroud has remained under the ownership of the House of Savoy ever since. It reposed in the Sainte Chapelle of Chambéry until 1578, and the only incident of note during that period was the fire that decimated the sacristy of that church on December 4, 1532. As the fire raged through the structure, the flames licked the silver casket in which the Shroud was folded. Risking death, two laymen—Filippo Lambert and Guglielmo Pussod—and two unidentified Franciscan priests rushed into the flaming church and rescued the Shroud. It did not, however, escape unharmed, since drops of molten silver from the casket had fallen on the linen and burned through its forty-eight folds.

In 1534 the damaged Shroud was taken to the monastery of Saint Clare, where the nuns applied the patches that still remain.

In 1578, Saint Charles Borromeo indicated his desire to make a pilgrimage to the Shroud. To spare the venerated saint the rigors of crossing the Alps, the duke of Savoy ordered the Shroud transferred to Turin, where, with the exception of a hiatus during the Second World War when it was removed to Monte Vergine for safekeeping, it has remained ever since.

As John Walsh points out, "The years of the relic's stay at Turin were relatively quiet ones, with its public showings very rare. At first it was displayed annually, but such frequent handling and exposure, it was feared, would damage it unnecessarily. The 1898 Exposition was only the sixth time that nineteenth-century eyes had looked upon it."

In 1900, Ulysse Chevalier, the twentieth century's most severe critic of the Shroud's authenticity, yet at the same time its most meticulous historian, wrote: "The history of the Shroud constitutes a protracted violation of the two virtues so often commended by our holy books, justice and truth." If such had not been the case, perhaps many of the controversies surrounding the Shroud could have been avoided. Unfortunately, that was not to be, and writing from the vantage point of time, one might also observe that Canon Chevalier was not the least of the offenders.

# VII

## *The Historians' Attack*

The publication of Secondo Pia's photographs of
1898 caused a worldwide sensation; millions of
Christians who had previously never even heard of
the Shroud now found themselves vitally concerned
with it; there was much talk of a miracle. It was in
this context that Canon Ulysse Chevalier entered the
proceedings.

Born in 1841, Chevalier had distinguished himself
at an early age. Entering the priesthood at twenty-
one, he soon accumulated honor upon honor until,
in 1883, he published his *Répetoire des Sources his-
toriques du moyen age,* an exhaustive study that
compiled almost all of the sources for the history of
the Middle Ages. One critic labeled Chevalier "the
most learned man in France and perhaps in the
entire world," and another called his book "the most
extraordinarily documented work a single man could
produce."

By the early 1900s and his entry into the Shroud
controversy, Chevalier was professor of ecclesiastical history at the Catholic Faculties of Lyon, and
one of the most formidable and respected historians
in the world. His position as a scholar was, in the
context of the Catholic world, liberal: it closely re-
sembled that of the Bollandists, the Belgian society

of Jesuit scholars to whom Chevalier repeatedly appealed in the course of the arguments over the Shroud, and whose approval of his position he regarded as decisive. The Bollandists had occupied themselves with church history for over two centuries. Their special interest was in the lives and legends of the saints, but the background and authenticity of relics were also the subject of their inquiries. They were among the pioneers and principal exponents of liberal Catholic scholarship, treading treacherous ground between Fundamentalist Catholics, to whom critical research into legends smacked of subversion and impiety, and rationalist historians, who dismissed the literature and practices of piety as absurd and unimportant. Like the Bollandists, Chevalier remained, to the end of the Shroud controversy, eager to free the church of grotesque beliefs and customs to make way for a more modern and more solid spirituality. In that context, it is no small wonder that he chose the Shroud, and the veneration accorded it, as a symbol of what he considered wrong with the church.

In Chevalier's first article on the Shroud—"Le Saint Suaire de Turin est-il l'original où une copie?" published in 1899—he drew attention to the case against authenticity made some years previously by Canon Charles Lalore (in *Revue catholique du diocèse de Troyes,* March 9 and 16, 1877). Lalore had examined most of the documents relevant to the Shroud, and had been content to summarize them: they proved that the Shroud had been regarded as a fraud in the fourteenth century, and to Lalore, this meant that it was still a fraud.

Chevalier merely transcribed, word for word, the arguments made by Lalore, and rested his case upon them. But he made his personal attitude to the question perfectly clear. He wrote, "The church is not afraid of the light; and in this case it will be seen that the light cast by written documents is brighter than the marvels of electricity."

From 1899 to 1903, Chevalier would publish nearly a dozen dissertations dealing with the Shroud, and while the latter of these would embroil him in technical and scientific arguments, his basic case would always go back to the documents, of which he found and published nearly fifty.

But what of these documents? What do they really prove? Virtually nothing, as we shall see.

The basic document used by Chevalier, as well as by most of the other historical critics of the Shroud's authenticity, is the letter from Pierre d'Arcis to Clement VII, in which d'Arcis sought, for once and for all, to stop the exposition of the Shroud at Lirey.

The key charge in the letter is d'Arcis' confirmation of the investigation undertaken by his predecessor, Henri de Poitiers, which proved that the Shroud was a forgery. Here, in translation, is the relevant portion of d'Arcis' letter:

The Lord Henry of Poitiers, of pious memory, then Bishop of Troyes, becoming aware of this, and urged by many prudent persons to take action, as indeed was his duty in the exercise of his ordinary jurisdiction, set himself earnestly to work to fathom the truth of this matter. For many theologians and other wise persons declared that this could not be the real shroud of our Lord, having the Savior's likeness thus imprinted upon it, since the Holy Gospel made no mention of any such imprint; while, if it had been true, it was quite unlikely that the holy Evangelists would have omitted to record

it, or that the fact should have remained hidden
until the present time. Eventually, after diligent
inquiry and examination, he discovered the fraud
and how the said cloth had been cunningly painted,
the truth being attested by the artist who had
painted it; to wit, that it was a work of human skill
and not miraculously wrought or bestowed. Accordingly, after taking mature counsel with wise
theologians and men of the law, seeing that he
neither ought nor could allow the matter to pass, he
began to institute formal proceedings against the
said Dean and his accomplices in order to root out
this false persuasion. They, seeing their wickedness
discovered, hid away the said cloth so that the
Ordinary could not find it, and they kept it hidden
afterwards for thirty-four years or thereabouts
down to the present year [1389].

The remainder of d'Arcis' letter is little more than
a sustained, yet completely unsubstantiated, attack
on the motives of those who would exhibit the
Shroud. As Father Wuenschel wrote in the *Ecclesiastical Review* in 1935:

Taken on its own merits, the memorial of Pierre
d'Arcis is untrustworthy, because it was written in
anger and betrays a strong bias against de Charny
and the Dean of Lirey. [Clement VII] himself, in
his rescript to de Charny and in his final decree,
declares that Pierre d'Arcis was angry with his
opponents for obtaining an indult to exhibit the
Shroud without his permission. He was still more
angry with them when they ignored his command
to withdraw the Shroud from public veneration,
and invoked the intervention of the king to prevent
him from taking action against them. And he was
hurt and humiliated when [Clement VII] upheld

his opponents and put him under silence in the rescript to the layman de Charny, leaving the outraged bishop to learn of this censure from common report. Pierre d'Arcis' memorial is a violent outburst over his grievances and a piece of special pleading in his own defense. He is so intemperate in his language, so bitter in his animus against those whom he accuses, so reckless in imputing to them the basest motives, that we cannot rely on his unsupported statement that they were guilty of the meanest kind of fraud.

Father Wuenschel's comments are generally accepted and echoed by most contemporary scholars who favor the Shroud's authenticity. If the d'Arcis letter had not been regarded as so important, we might leave it at that, dismissing it as inconclusive and one-sided evidence at best. But even if the letter were a vicious, self-serving attack on d'Arcis' enemies, might there not be some substance to his charges?

If Henri de Poitiers conducted an investigation of the Shroud, there is only the d'Arcis letter to say so. Throughout the exchanges, d'Arcis never produced a single piece of supportive evidence. Certainly d'Arcis, as de Poitiers' successor, would have had access to any such records, and had they existed, he undoubtedly would have produced them. Neither is there any record of the investigation in the work of Nicholas Camuzat, the historian of the diocese of Troyes, and had such an investigation actually taken place, it is unlikely that it would have escaped the historian's attention. Finally, neither Canon Chevalier nor any of his fellow critics have ever been able to unearth any documents to support d'Arcis' charges. Given Chevalier's uncontested aptitude for bringing to light precisely such documents, as well as the vengeance with which he sought to refute the authenticity of the Shroud, it is inconceivable that even the slightest fragment of support for his cause would have eluded him.

According to Pierre d'Arcis, the exposition of the Shroud which caused de Poitiers to take action against the canons of Lirey would have taken place in 1355, "or thereabouts." But on May 28, 1356, de Poitiers issued his confirmation of the establishment of the church at Lirey, to which he gave his unqualified and lavish blessings. That document does exist, and in it not a word is said about the Shroud, about the investigation, or about any other relic. Are we to believe, then, that a bishop who had been at such loggerheads with local church officials just the year before would issue such a laudatory document? Hardly.

Even if we accept the impreciseness of d'Arcis' "or thereabouts" dating, the whole alleged affair just cannot have taken place in any year in which there were not other such glaring conflicts. Problems like these, however, Canon Chevalier chose to ignore.

All of the other documents that Chevalier enlisted to his cause were largely irrelevent or had even less merit than the d'Arcis letter. Those dealing with the foundation of the church at Lirey made no mention of the Shroud at all, and while we may find this perplexing, there are no satisfactory conclusions we can draw from them. Most of the other documents were produced as a result of the d'Arcis letter, and are proof of nothing other than the rough chronology of the Shroud from the time it was made public as a possession of the de Charny family.

Unfortunately, however, those who sought to

challenge the didactic conclusions of Canon Chevalier at the time could match him neither in intellect nor wit. His imposing reputation coupled with his brilliant scholastic fire dance on the facts—or lack thereof—had a chilling effect on serious interest in the Shroud. Chevalier received a gold medal for his exposé of the spurious relic, and most reputable scholars wrote the Shroud off as one of the more bizarre curiosities of church history and went on to more serious endeavors.

If Chevalier had not done enough damage, enter now, again in the early 1900s, the Reverend Herbert Thurston, a feisty English Jesuit who liked nothing better than an intellectual public brawl. From the vantage point of time, Thurston's dissertations on the Shroud—which very closely followed the lines of Chevalier's—emerge as little more than severely dated footnotes to the story. But because of his attacks generally, and specifically his critical dismissal of the Shroud in the then current edition of the influential *Catholic Encyclopaedia,* Thurston almost single-handedly managed to stifle discourse on the Shroud in the English-speaking world for many years. (Prior to the televised exposition of the Shroud in November 1973, and the subsequent publicity, it was estimated that only one out of twenty people in the world knew anything at all about the Shroud.

It has been stated that the historian is the worst enemy of the Shroud. Certainly some historians have been, if only because their attacks so severely curtailed serious academic study for so many years.

But do the objections of the historians have any merit at all?

It has been charged that the Shroud has no documented, uninterrupted history from its mention in the Gospels until its surfacing as a possession of the de Charny family in the fourteenth century. It is possible that Dr. Wilson's study of the Edessan Image will substantially reduce this "lost millennium"; but even if it does not, the Shroud does exist, and it is its own most impressive evidence. On it is the image of a crucified man. Analysis of the cloth indicates that it could date to the time of Jesus. Does its lack of pedigree, then, make it any less real? It does not; it merely means that history, in this case, can offer support neither to authenticity nor fabrication.

It has been charged that Pierre d'Arcis' letter to Clement VII fully proves that the Shroud is a fake. As we have seen, it does no such thing, and as evidence it is virtually worthless without supporting documentation. But even if the documentation did exist—if Henri de Poitiers had conducted an investigation, and if an artist had testified that he painted the Shroud—we would still be left with the plaguing question of how that artist accomplished a feat so complicated and requiring so much knowledge that, to this date, it cannot be duplicated by any process man has ever known—painting least of all.

Finally, it has been charged that even those involved in the controversy over the Shroud in the fourteenth and fifteenth centuries—including members of the de Charny family—did not themselves believe in its authenticity. Summoned forth as evidence are all the documents which refer to the Shroud as a "representation" of the burial cloth of

Christ. This is, of course, the weakest argument of all, for if twentieth-century experts of many and varied disciplines have not yet been able to satisfactorily determine the authenticity or fraudulence of the Shroud, then certainly the unqualified opinions of the Middle Ages, affected by all the misconceptions and prejudices of that time, have no merit whatsoever.

History, then, will not settle the case of the Shroud for either side, and if there are to be satisfactory answers to the centuries-old puzzle, we must turn to science, to the coldly rational examination of the only real document of importance—the Shroud itself.

# VIII

## The Believer and the Agnostic: Two Scientists in Search of the Truth

While Canon Chevalier was basking in the glory of his largely unchallenged scholarship and accepting kudos from all quarters, there were two men, at least, who had not forgotten about the Shroud. To the contrary, they had taken the study of it from the realms of the church and the historian into the glaring light of the scientific laboratory. Chevalier's earlier pronouncement aside, that light would prove bright indeed.

Like Secondo Pia, whose remarkable photographs had thrust the study of the Shroud into the modern age, Paul Joseph Vignon seemed admirably suited for the task at hand. While published records of Vignon's personal life are scant, John Walsh's account in *The Shroud,* based on interviews with members of Vignon's family, does offer some interesting insights. Born to wealth in Lyon, France, in 1865, Vignon was able to pursue a multiplicity of interests free from the need to produce an income. Not the least of these was his love of mountain climbing, which he followed vigorously until 1895, when a physical and nervous breakdown brought on by his relentless challenge of the most dangerous peaks forced him to exchange his athletic prowess for more sedate, if no less challenging, pursuits.

As Walsh ironically points out, on some of his mountain forays, "Vignon had for companion another dedicated mountaineer, a young Italian priest named Achille Ratti. Thus, the lure of the mountains had brought together, briefly, the two men who were to become the leading modern advocates of the Shroud of Turin. Years later they met again in a private-audience room at the Vatican—Vignon as the moving spirit in the scientific study of the relic, and Ratti as the learned Pope Pius XI, who believed wholeheartedly in its authenticity."

Vignon's illness provided another fortuitous circumstance; for during his convalescence in Switzerland, he would take up painting as therapy, and would soon find himself an accomplished artist, displaying his works in a distinguished Paris salon.

About a year after his recovery, Vignon met Yves Delage. Delage was one of France's foremost scientists, an internationally acclaimed zoologist, associate director of the Laboratory for Research in Experimental Zoology, a professor at the Sorbonne, a director of the Museum of Natural History and a member of the powerful and distinguished French Academy of Sciences. Eleven years Vignon's senior, Delage was also a well-known agnostic whose frequently stated views on most religious matters were quite dim. Vignon was a practicing Catholic.

If their disparate religious leanings were ever an issue between the two men, there is no record of it, and it is likely that they served as perfect foils to each other during the time they would devote to the

Shroud. And unlike Chevalier, each man was prepared to drop any preconceived notions the moment he entered the laboratory. What would emerge from their study would be the truth, or the closest scientific experimentation could come to it.

Shortly after their first meeting Vignon's interest in biology, for which he had been professionally trained, was reawakened by Delage, and the younger man soon joined his mentor on the staff of *The Biological Year,* a magazine Delage had founded and edited. Later, Vignon would become Delage's personal assistant, as well as take up his own instructorship in biology at the Sorbonne.

Vignon had seen Pia's photographs of the Shroud —most literate men of the time had—but after the publicity surrounding Chevalier's attacks, he, as others had done, dismissed the whole issue as unworthy of further pursuit. Not so Delage. As a scientist, he could not remove the power and reality of the images from his mind; his family told John Walsh that he was "disturbed" by them. To the agnostic Delage, Chevalier's historical "proof" of the Shroud's forgery must have seemed just one more church-related fallacy of the type Delage so loved to explode. If the explosion of this one might placate critics of his agnosticism, at least he would once again demonstrate that the truth of religious questions would be better served by unbiased scientific exploration than by the self-serving and disputable contentions of exegetes and scholars.

Thus, at Delage's instigation, Vignon and several other scientists set about to investigate the Shroud. Was it indeed a painting, a forgery, as Chevalier and others insisted? Or was it something else? If it were something else, would there be a natural, physical explanation that could be duplicated, or at least determined, in a laboratory? Was the figure imprinted on the Shroud the historical personage of Jesus?

The details of Vignon's experiments and findings are to be found in his book *The Shroud of Christ*, published in 1902. (Few copies of the English translation remain; one is in the collection of the New York Public Library.)

Vignon first went to visit Secondo Pia, who explained exactly how he had taken his photographs and gave Vignon several of his best copies. If Vignon had previously questioned whether Pia had in some way faked the negative image, these thoughts were soon dispelled, for Vignon also located several other photographs—of poor quality, granted—but taken by others and corroborating the negativity of the Shroud image.

As an artist, Vignon realized that the reality of the negative image was equal or superior to the best paintings of the Renaissance. But even supposing that such a picture *could* have been painted in the fourteenth century, why should it have been painted in the negative? The very concept of negativity was unknown until photography was invented, and a fourteenth-century forger would surely have been working to produce something acceptable and believable in his own time, and not for twentieth-century scientists. In addition, the position of the nail—in the wrist rather than in the palm of the hand—was in conflict with artistic tradition, and the nakedness of the figure would surely have shocked the sensibilities of the faithful.

But if the Shroud had not been painted in the negative, could it not have been reproduced by traditional application of colors to the linen, and the image reversal perhaps have been induced by a chemical transformation of the colors at some later date? Some critics did in fact make this charge, but records as to what the image had looked like in earlier times were so sparse that no conclusions could be drawn from them. To refute the possibility of chemical transformation, Vignon himself dutifully cited a fresco in the Upper Church of Saint Francis at Assisi. The painting is attributed to Cimabue, and its light values have in fact been reversed by the action of sulfur on the lead base of the paints. But Vignon claimed justly that the image of the Shroud is monochromatic, and had not been colored by the application of paint. Thus there could be no question of two colors changing in opposite directions with the passage of time or, as many had thought, in the heat of the fire at Chambéry in 1532.

Still anxious to dismiss the possibility of the Shroud being a painting, Vignon obtained pieces of linen closely approximating the weave and thickness of the Shroud. These he painted with both oils and watercolors, using the lightest wash that would produce definable images. After the paintings had dried, folding them or rolling them up produced the results one might expect: the paint crumbled and fell off. If the Shroud were the work of an artist, Vignon concluded, then it must have been made with a wash of dye that diffused into the cloth itself, and such dyes would not have been subject to chemical changes that could produce the negative characteristics of the image.

But if the imprints on the Shroud were not the work of an artist, could they have been produced by direct contact with a human body? Vignon donned a false beard, covered himself with fine red chalk, and lay down on a table in his laboratory. His assistants coated a strip of linen with albumen to pick up the chalk impression and draped the cloth over him. The imprints produced in this way were only partial, for the parts of the body that did not touch the sheet left no marks at all; they were also grossly distorted. The face, over which the sheet had been smoothed down, left no imprint comparable in accuracy and detail to that on the Shroud.

Vignon and his assistants repeated the experiment several times, with variations in method, with greater care, but at no time could they produce a satisfactory image. The image on the Shroud is perfect in its reproduction of anatomical detail; what Vignon got were nothing more than crude, distorted caricatures.

If Vignon and his associates, with all the artistic and scientific knowledge of the twentieth century, could not produce a negative image on cloth by any of these methods, is it conceivable that some fourteenth-century forger could have produced a work that confounds us even today?

Vignon believed that he had successfully discounted the prospect of forgery, but could he go further to prove authenticity? To do so would require a scientifically acceptable explanation for the negative image. It was at this point that he began hypothesizing that the imprints were formed by some physico-chemical process that could approximate the qualities of photography. Perhaps, Vignon reasoned, the body could have actually projected the image, which varied in intensity depending upon the distance of projection, onto the Shroud which had somehow been sensitized to react with much the same results as a photographic plate.

Working with a friend, René Colson, a professor of physics at the Ecole Polytechnique in Paris, Vignon tried to determine the practicality of his unique idea. From reading the Gospels he believed that the Shroud had been anointed with myrrh and aloes, common aromatics that were frequently used in burial rites. In reading further Colson found an ancient recipe that indicated the myrrh and aloes were pounded with olive oil to form a paste which was then smeared on the burial cloth. An emulsion of aloes in olive oil would yield aloetine, and a cloth soaked in aloetine would brown under the influence of alkaline vapors. Now the two scientists had their sensitized cloth, their "photographic plate." All they had to find would be the origin of the alkaline vapors.

Vignon and Colson knew that vaporized ammonia can project images—they had performed tests to be sure—and when they consulted with chemists, they learned that a body in a crisis of pain emits what is called morbid sweat. They also learned that the body produces a chemical compound called urea, which accumulates in the body fluids as a by-product of protein metabolism. Normal sweat contains some urea, but morbid sweat is highly charged with it. Upon fermentation, urea becomes carbonate of ammonia, and carbonate of ammonia gives off exactly the kind of alkaline vapors that could produce an image like that on the Shroud.

The two scientists went back into the laboratory, and fresh experiments lent substance to their hypothesis. Their best results were obtained by moistening a plaster cast of a hand with ammonia, inserting it into a kid glove and exposing it to a cloth soaked with aloetine. The print thus obtained showed the mass of each finger, but was graduated with such delicacy that no lines of division appeared. Experiments with larger objects, such as plaster heads, were far less successful, mainly because merely moistening plaster with ammonia produced too fast and free a flow of vapors. But it would have been impossible to absolutely duplicate the conditions under which the Shroud's image had been formed, and even the moderate success of Vignon's experiments assured him that he was correct.

He had a burial shroud sensitized by some combination of spices and oils to act as a photographic plate. He had, in the crucifixion of Jesus, a body tortured and wracked with pain. And he had a feasible chemical process that could project an image on the sensitized cloth. Paul Joseph Vignon had eliminated the most perplexing mystery of the Shroud—he knew how its image had been formed. His findings would become known as the vaporograph theory. Vignon would go further in his investigations before making his discovery public, but the vaporographic theory alone would be his most impressive achievement.

On April 21, 1902, Yves Delage stood before the crowded assembly of the august French Academy of Sciences. As John Walsh writes:

The French Academy was, without doubt, the foremost scientific body in the world at the time, and this room was steeped in long tradition. Statues and paintings of the greats of French science and literature peered down from the wooden paneling, emphasizing a sense of continuity with the past that was almost tangible. Only a decade before, one of these weekly meetings had witnessed the first presentation of the basic electrical phenomenon that had led to wireless telegraphy. Interestingly it was before a similar gathering in 1839, that the technique of photography itself was first given to the world by Daguerre. There still lingered in the atmosphere dramatic memories of Louis Pasteur, especially of the famous meeting at which he had announced his vaccine for rabies. That had been nearly fifteen years before—the last time the hall had accommodated such a crush of listeners.

Delage, aware of the singular importance of the occasion, began reading the paper that he and Vignon had prepared. After discussing the history and properties of the Shroud, he detailed the step-by-step research and experiments of Vignon and his colleagues, work which Delage had overseen and approved until its conclusion. Science had shown the Shroud was not, could not be, a painting; science had demonstrated the Shroud was not some other kind of forgery; science had even determined how the image was formed.

Now Delage went on: "Let us add to this, that, in order for the image to have formed itself without being ultimately destroyed, it was necessary that the corpse remain in the Shroud at least twenty-four hours, the amount of time needed for the formation of the image, and at the most several days, after which putrefaction sets in, which destroys the image and finally the Shroud." Delage paused, aware of the impact of his next statement, particularly coming from him. "Tradition—more or less apocryphal, I would say—tells us that this is precisely what happened to Christ; dead on Friday and—disappeared —on Sunday. The man of the Shroud was Christ."

There were more details, to be sure, but Delage's conclusions had been stated, firmly and with absolute conviction. As a man of science, as an agnostic, he believed in the authenticity of the Shroud.

Delage's presentation caused a major sensation in scientific, intellectual and religious circles. The secretary of the Academy refused to print in the *Comptes rendus* (the official proceedings of the Academy) any part of the presentation that asserted the image on the Shroud was that of Jesus. A secret committee of the Academy rejected Delage's request that a more complete investigation of the Shroud be instigated under its auspices. And the international press took up the story with such fervor that the earlier attention accorded Secondo Pia's photographs seemed pale in comparison.

Vignon and Delage were attacked one day and praised the next. Years later, some of the criticism that would be leveled would come from other serious scientists who had done their own research; but at the time, most critics reacted hysterically, grasping at any and every contradictory theory they could summon.

Delage, somewhat taken aback by the savagery of the controversy he had unleashed, expressed himself once more, in a letter to *Revue Scientifique*. He said, in part:

> I willingly recognize that none of these given arguments offers the features of an irrefutable demonstration; but it must be recognized that their sum constitutes a bundle of imposing probabilities,

some of which are very close to being proven. . . . A religious question has been needlessly injected into a problem which in itself is purely scientific, with the result that feelings have run high, and reason has been led astray. If, instead of Christ, there were a question of some person like a Sargon, an Achilles or one of the pharaohs, no one would have thought of making any objections. . . . I have been faithful to the true spirit of science in treating this question, intent only on the truth, not concerned in the least whether it would affect the interests of any religious party. . . . I recognize Christ as a historical personage and I see no reason why anyone should be scandalized that there still exist material traces of his earthly life.

Several months later, Delage returned to other scientific pursuits. For him, the Shroud was only one episode in a long and distinguished career. Vignon, however, would spend the rest of his life studying the Shroud.

# IX

## *The Second Set of Photographs*

For thirty-three years, from June 2, 1898 until May 3, 1931, throughout the height of the public controversy over the Shroud, the venerable cloth itself had remained hidden, locked in its silver casket above the altar of the Royal Chapel of Turin.

All those who had joined in the controversy during this period had no opportunity to see the Shroud itself, but had worked from copies of Secondo Pia's photograph. Following Yves Delage's presentation of Vignon's findings and the publication of Vignon's book, Canon Chevalier severely rebuked Vignon for invoking the methods of the natural sciences in dealing with an object he had never seen. But of course the indefatigable historian had recognized no such compunctions when promoting his own theories.

Father Thurston, while praising the scientific rigor of Vignon's investigation, charged that Pia's black-and-white photograph could be misleading as to the issue of the color of the actual image and the possibility of some sort of color reversal, if nothing else. Thus, until the historical question was settled, Vignon's theory was only of academic value. Since, in his own mind, Thurston had already settled the historical question in favor of a fourteenth-century forgery, he was merely giving Vignon's work a polite brush-off; but at least he had attempted to deal with it.

Although any number of petitions had requested that the Shroud be made available for study during this period, all had either been rejected or ignored. If certain individuals of the church hierarchy or members of the royal House of Savoy had looked at it, for whatever reasons, there are no records of their impressions. In 1931, however, the king's son, Crown Prince Humbert, was to be married, and the House of Savoy would celebrate the joyous national occasion with the public exposition of their most prized possession.

As in 1898, millions of the faithful would endure long lines to see it, and in addition to the exposition, the king would respond—somewhat gingerly—to the many petitions for greater scrutiny. Scientists still would not be allowed to study the Shroud firsthand, but the king did grant permission for a new set of photographs to be taken. Needless to say, photography had become quite sophisticated since Secondo Pia's time, and the availability of a wide variety of modern cameras and equipment would insure technical perfection. As a photographer, the then cardinal of Turin, Maurilio Fossati, chose Giuseppe Enrie, who was regarded as one of Italy's best. Joining Enrie as consultants were Secondo Pia and Paul Vignon, the two men who had done the most toward uncovering the mystery of the Shroud at the time.

Enrie made a number of photographs, the most important of which are a three-section blowup of the entire Shroud, a life-sized reproduction of the face, a smaller shot of the shoulders and back and a seven-to-one enlargement of the area around the wound in the left hand.

All of Enrie's photographs were taken in the presence of a large number of witnesses; all were developed immediately in a special sacristy dark-room; and all were compared with the Shroud by a panel of experts who pronounced them faithful in every detail to their subject. To guard against a repeat of the charges of fakery that had earlier been leveled at Secondo Pia, a set of affidavits, sworn before a notary, were drawn up, attesting that the photographs were genuine and official.

The new photographs confirmed the legitimacy of Pia's work, and portrayed all the aspects of the Shroud with greater clarity and detail. The blowup of the wrist area supported Vignon's contention that there was no evidence of paint or other coloring applied to the surface of the cloth; the image, how-ever it had been made, was subtly diffused into the cloth itself. The same photograph afforded textile authorities the basis with which to classify the cloth as one that could have been common in Jesus' time, and one that was not in use in Europe at any time that the Shroud could have been forged there. In addition, copies of Enrie's photographs were soon dispatched to every corner of the world, and became the basis for the great body of scientific study that has continued to the present. (The photographs of the Shroud in this book are copies made from the originals by one of Enrie's successors, and so close-ly are they protected that anyone using them for reproduction must certify that they will not be re-touched or altered in any way.)

Even after the carefully witnessed sessions during which Enrie took and developed the photographs, and after the affidavits of experts attesting to their true affinity to the Shroud in clarity and detail, some scholars have still maintained that the photographs are not an adequate basis for legitimate scientific study of the Shroud. And while there is not a scientist who would not have given his right arm to have been able to work from the actual cloth, the arguments of the critics on this point are completely without merit. None of the studies which are accepted as legitimate have exceeded the bounds of the photographic evidence, and all those involved admit that not until a number of sophisticated tests have been conducted on the actual cloth will there be any conclusive determination of its authenticity. But, as Werner Bulst puts it:

> Photography is one of the most important tools of investigation used by modern science to approach an object. For photography reproduces any object, in the realm of the visible world, with strict fidelity to nature. In the case of a practically two-dimensional object, like a cloth, the object stands out all the more perfectly in a photograph. Furthermore, photography makes it possible to see much that cannot be detected at all by the human eye, through enlargement, intensification of contrast, use of color filters and properly sensitized film [or plates]. In the case of the Cloth of Turin, it was precisely this that first chanced upon the negative characteristics of the image on the linen fabric. Photography likewise enables anyone at all to examine and test the result wherever he wants. Furthermore, theologians should leave it to scientists to judge the principles and methods of scientific investigation. To date, the latter have expressed no misgivings about using the photographs

115

of Enrie. Concerning the validity of scientific investigation based on photographs, the author has repeatedly questioned specialists, particularly in the field of forensic medicine and chemistry, the field of the history of textiles and art, and in every instance this procedure has received unequivocal approval.

In fact, forensic medicine, which has something vital to say on the possible authenticity of the Cloth of Turin, makes extensive use of photographs nowadays, and precisely by this very means settles a high percentage of its cases. But rarely does it have at its disposal photographs of the size and quality taken by Enrie. The expert in forensic medicine frequently meets in his work with a situation similar to that found till now in the study of the Cloth of Turin: for extrinsic reasons he is unable to handle the substance of the article to be examined, so that, among other things, chemical analysis is precluded. And yet, despite this, reliable results are often achieved.

As the exposition of 1931 drew to a close, study was beginning on Enrie's photographs that would yield results far more compelling than anything previously ventured.

# X

## Dr. Pierre Barbet: A Surgeon at Calvary

Following the 1931 exposition, a number of men representing many fields of knowledge began intensive studies of the Shroud, working primarily from Enrie's photographs. Not the least of these was Dr. Pierre Barbet, whose medical and anatomical experiments would provide the most comprehensive and authoritative evidence for the authenticity of the Shroud yet compiled.

Of all those men who have contributed so significantly to the story of the Shroud, the details of Barbet's personal life are the least known, and serve as little more than a fragmentary footnote to the impressive work he did. His professional qualifications, however, are firmly established and impeccable. Born in 1883, he was surgeon general of the renowned Saint Joseph's Hospital in Paris for thirty-five years, and was particularly admired for the speed and proficiency of his surgical skills. In addition, he was a formidable expert on anatomy, and had taught that subject for many years.

In 1931 Dr. Barbet was approached by a clergyman friend, one Father Armailhac, with a set of Enrie's photographs. The priest sought the opinion of a surgeon and anatomist. Could a medical authority provide the answers that had eluded the theologians and historians? Paul Vignon had tried earlier to deal with some of the medical questions, but Pia's photographs—from which Vignon had worked—lacked the clarity and detail of Enrie's and while Vignon had advanced some opinions, they were not generally considered authoritative. Barbet's would be.

Barbet's studies lasted some fifteen years, and in the end touched on every aspect of the Shroud; but his most important work—the physiological and anatomical investigations—was conducted between 1932 and 1935. In 1933 Pope Pius XI declared a holy year, and petitioned the king of Italy for a new exposition of the Shroud. During that exposition Barbet was allowed to observe the actual cloth at close range, thus confirming and adding to the knowledge he had already gleaned from the photographs.

During the course of his studies Barbet would publish a number of pamphlets and articles. One of these, "The Corporal Passion of Jesus Christ," published in 1940, presented a vivid, graphic re-creation of the Passion, based on Barbet's experiments. By and large, however, his earlier works were written for his sophisticated medical colleagues and were beyond the comprehension of the average layman. Realizing this, in 1950 he published *La Passion de N.-S. Jésus Christ selon le Chirugien,* which covered the whole of his studies and simplified them as much as possible. The English translation, titled *A Doctor at Calvary,* was published in 1953, and is probably the best known of all books on the Shroud. (While indispensable to serious sindonologists, the book is still quite difficult, and its translation, I am told by authorities, is not only bad, but in places misrepresents what Barbet intended to say. In addition, some of Barbet's historical and archaeological findings are not nearly as authoritative as his medical studies, and should be approached with caution.)

To deal with Barbet's findings as clearly and as simply as possible, it is best to take them one point at a time, not necessarily in the order he arrived at them or presented them in his book.

## The Distinction between the Body Images and the Bloodstains

At the exposition of 1933, Dr. Barbet was able to see at first hand the pronounced differences between the appearance of the body images and the bloodstains. He had already amassed a solid block of evidence from the photographs, but they were in black and white, and his study of the distinctively different colorations on the actual cloth provided reinforcement to his position. First he noted the mistlike quality of the body images, so diffused into the cloth that there are no lines of demarcation, contours or shadows, just subtle variations in the light and shade of the brownish stains. In contrast, the bloodstains are much richer in color and have a more precise outline. Barbet also noted that the bloodstains appear thicker at the edges, and that in some places they are "surrounded by an aureole of a much paler color, like a sort of halo." These "halos," he believed, were produced by the serum which separates from the cellular mass of blood as it congeals. Every other detail of the bloodstains on the Shroud matched what Barbet knew to be true in nature. Further, he pointed out that on the Shroud the bloodstains appear as positive images, while the body appears as a negative (see Plate 6). Thus, he concluded, the blood which flowed from the wounds coagulated on the skin and was transferred to the cloth by direct contact, yielding the positive images, as it should. The body images, however, had been "projected" in some way, and appeared as negative images.

That a fourteenth-century artist could have duplicated the complexities of blood coagulation so perfectly, without making a single mistake, was beyond Barbet's comprehension as a doctor. And he seriously doubted that even the most skilled medical man could have faked it without being detected.

## The Preliminary Sufferings

In studying all of the marks which appear on the Shroud, Barbet was able to isolate and identify those wounds caused prior to the actual crucifixion. In every case his medical diagnosis corresponded exactly with the record of the Passion as reported in the Gospels or determined by archaeological investigation.

On the face of the Shroud Dr. Barbet found a number of excoriations, wounds in which the skin is broken. These are particularly noticeable on the right side of the face, and seem to have been caused by blows with a stick approximately 1¾ inches in diameter. The most prominent of these is below the right eye-socket, but there are others on the left cheek and the lower lip; and Barbet also detected a fractured nose.

All over the body, from the shoulders to the lower part of the legs and primarily visible on the dorsal image, are the wounds produced by the scourging with the Roman *flagrum*. Barbet noted that all these wounds have a uniform shape and size, and appear as two circles (the balls of lead or bone) joined by a line (the thong that held the balls). He counted as many as one hundred and twenty of these, and reasoned that the wounds represented sixty strokes with a double-thonged *flagrum*. He also pointed out that additional strokes might have been administered, but on the Shroud the only ones visible are those which actually broke the flesh. He further reasoned, from the angle of the wounds (which are not the same on both sides of the body), that they were inflicted by two different men.

From the ring of bloodstains that encircle the head, Barbet determined that the crown of thorns was a definite reality. There is no image on the Shroud left by the top of the head; blank cloth separates the frontal and dorsal images. But if the crown of thorns were a cap rather than a circlet, as is believed, why would there not be bloodstains or even a faint image? Barbet believed that the top of the head was covered by a handkerchief joined under the chin, the purpose of which would have been to keep the mouth closed in death against the forces of rigor mortis. Thus the handkerchief absorbed the blood before it could be transferred to the Shroud, and also prevented the formation of the body image at this point.

On the back of the head is evidence of the most blood. Barbet reasoned this as perfectly natural, since in the throes of agony Jesus' head would have frequently pitched back against the cross, making those wounds larger and deeper. Again based on his surgeon's knowledge of how blood flows and coagulates, Barbet concluded that every mark produced by the crown of thorns is absolutely true to nature, and could not possibly have been painted or faked.

Next he turned to three broad patches of wounds: at the level of the left shoulder blade, at the knees and across the right shoulder. These, he believed, were caused directly or indirectly by Jesus' carrying of the crossbeam up the rugged terrain to Calvary. The crossbeam would have been heavy and roughly hewn, and during the long walk up Calvary, it would have rubbed and chafed violently across the right shoulder on which it rested. Every time Jesus fell, the length of the crossbeam behind him would have struck his back a glancing, chafing blow, which would further be inflamed as he struggled to rise under his burden. Also as Jesus fell, the scattered, jagged rocks on the road could not have helped but scratch and cut into the flesh of his knees.

Taking this thesis even further, Barbet pointed to the so-called Holy Coat of Argenteuil. This cloak, housed in the parish church of Argenteuil, France, and believed to have been brought there by Charlemagne, is traditionally accepted as "the seamless garment of Christ," worn during his ordeal before the crucifixion, and for which the Roman soldiers cast lots after the crucifixion.

In 1934 the coat was photographed, using infrared equipment, by Gérard Cordonnier, a friend of Barbet and member of the French Regiment of Engineers. On his photograph, what are believed to be bloodstains show up in the same places as Barbet identified them on the Shroud. The accuracy of their placement was further confirmed by reproducing the stains from the coat on a tunic of the same dimensions, and placing the tunic on a man about six feet in height, which is believed to be Jesus' height as determined by the images on the Shroud. Again Barbet's theory was upheld. (It should be noted here that this author has not been able to find corroborating evidence of this comparative experiment, or any evidence other than traditional affirmations that the Holy Coat of Argenteuil is itself authentic. Certainly, however, when the Shroud is finally tested with sophisticated instruments, this coat should be put to those same tests, if only as a supportive measure in the authentication of the Shroud.)

## The Wounds in the Hands

According to Gospel descriptions, artistic tradition and popular belief, the wounds in Jesus' hands were caused by the nails driven through the palms. But the evidence of the Shroud, and of physical reality, contradicts these sources, and it is precisely with regard to these wounds that Dr. Barbet made one of his most important discoveries.

On the Shroud, the left hand completely overlaps the right wrist, so that only one wound is visible—through the left wrist. The wound is clear, having formed a round image from which there are several streams of blood. Similar trickles of blood appear on the right forearm, which is visible.

To prove that crucifixion could not possibly have been successful by nailing the palms, Barbet took an amputated arm from a cadaver, drove a nail through the palm and suspended a weight of eighty-eight pounds from the elbow. This weight he took to be approximately half that of a man six feet tall. Within minutes, the force of the weight had ripped completely through the palm, and Barbet's whole experiment crashed to the floor. But this was dead weight, still and undisturbed. In actual circumstances, the writhing contortions of the victim would have produced far greater force, exercised in a number of directions. But if the nails were not driven through the palms, then where, and how?

The wrist is a complex of bones and muscles, and Barbet could not at first figure out how a nail could have been inserted. It would have to be in a place that would secure the body and at the same time be free of bones that would deflect the nail. Comparing the position of the wound on the Shroud to anatomical reality, he found that the wound was centered directly behind the ridge of the upper palm, at the most prominent bending fold of the wrist (see Plates 12 and 13). In exactly that spot is a fleshy space, quite small, which is bounded by four major bones. This gap is called by anatomists the Space of Destot, after the French physician who located and identified it. But the space was small—too small, thought Barbet—to allow the uninterrupted journey of the nail.

Again using the arm of a cadaver, Dr. Barbet carefully marked the spot of the wound and drove a nail through it. He repeated the experiment again and again, and each time he got the same results: the nail passed through easily, finding the natural channel by slightly moving aside the surrounding bones, breaking none, and merely enlarging the space. Thus surrounded by bones and ligaments, the nail would have held firm against even greater pressure than a dying man could muster.

Certainly, Barbet mused, experienced executioners would be no strangers to this anatomical intrica-
cy, which must have seemed perfectly suited to their
bizarre needs. But for a fourteenth-century forger to
have such knowledge? Impossible, unless he were a
skilled surgeon, centuries ahead of his time.

Dr. Barbet knew then where and how the nails
had been driven, but his experiments also yielded a
surprise for which even he, with all his medical
experience and sophistication, was not prepared. On
the Shroud, although the backs of both hands are
clearly visible, neither thumb can be seen (see Plate
11). Many critics of the Shroud's authenticity had
pointed to this anomaly in declaring the Shroud a
fraud. Such an "error" could not possibly have
happened in reality; this had to be the bumbling of
the forger, they said.

But every time Barbet had driven a nail into the
freshly amputated wrist of a cadaver, he observed
that "at the moment when the nail went through the
soft anterior parts, the palm being upwards, the
thumb would bend sharply and would be exactly
facing the palm. . . ." In dissection of the arms,
Barbet learned that the trunk of the median nerve
was always seriously injured by the penetration of the
nail. And this "mechanical stimulation" of the median nerve—which is also the motor, or sensory,
nerve—caused the contraction of the thenar muscle,
which controls the movement of the thumb.

Could a forger have known that? asked Barbet.
And even if he had, would he have dared to portray
this obscure physiological quirk that would not be
identified and understood for centuries? Hardly.

Not content to stop there, Barbet next studied the
blood which had flowed from the wrist wounds. The

shape of the bloodstains bothered him, for it seemed that the blood had flowed in several distinctly different directions. From a careful study of the angles of the flow, he determined that the body had alternately taken two different positions on the cross (see Plate 10). His explanation of this is both complex and graphic.

When the wrists were nailed to the crossbeams, the arms were outstretched at a ninety-degree angle to the vertical post of the cross. As soon as these nails were in place, the executioners removed their support of the body and, hanging only from the wrist nails, it sagged, causing the arms to drop from their perpendicular angle to one of sixty-five degrees. It was in this position that the blood flowed from the wrist toward the elbow in a more-or-less linear path; and since the blood flow appears primarily in this direction, it would seem that this was the predominant position of the body on the cross. However, some trickles of blood also flowed at angles of between sixty-eight and seventy degrees, indicating that the body had raised itself slightly from time to time, thus moving the arms back toward their original horizontal position.

Dr. Barbet postulated these angles by charting the bloodstains on the Shroud, later working them out on geometric graphs and confirming them by experimenting with a cadaver. He knew what had happened and only needed to discover why. The why is part of his theory of exactly how Jesus died.

*The Causes of Death*

As has already been noted, when Jesus' wrists were nailed to the cross and the support given by the executioners then removed, his body sagged, and his entire weight hung from the wrists. His arms were thus stretched obliquely (at sixty-five degree angles) above his head. Dr. Barbet computed the weight that dragged on each wrist to be two hundred-forty pounds of pressure. Then the feet were nailed, the legs bent in a slightly flexed position.

In this position, which was the most common in crucifixion, the sides would be relatively immobile; exhalation would be greatly hindered, and the victim would have the sensation of progressive suffocation. The heart would have to work harder, its beats becoming faster and weaker.

Cramps would begin in the forearms, then in the arms, and would finally spread to the lower limbs and the trunk. The lungs would be filled with air but unable to expel it. Thus the normal oxygenation of the circulating blood would not take place, and asphyxiation would begin. The victim would be affected as surely and as drastically as if he were being violently strangled. This same condition, Dr. Barbet explained, is produced by tetanus, through the intoxication of the nerve centers. The combination of symptoms of general contraction is thus called "tetany." Asphyxiation and tetany would cause rapid death.

If such was the case, how then, asked Dr. Barbet, could victims of crucifixion "escape for the moment from these cramps and this asphyxia, so that they survived for several hours, even for two or three days? This could only be done by relieving the dragging on the hands, which seems to be the initial and determining cause of the whole phenomenon."

There was a way.

Using his feet as a fulcrum, the victim could lift his body and bring his arms back toward their original horizontal position. With the weight of the body thus supported by the muscles in the legs and the nails through the feet, "the dragging on the hands would then be greatly reduced; the cramps would be lessened and the asphyxia would disappear for the moment, through the renewal of the respiratory movements. Then the fatigue of the lower legs would supervene, which would force the crucified to drop again, and bring on a fresh attack of asphyxia. The whole agony was thus spent in an alternation of sagging and then of straightening the body, of asphyxia and respiration."

Once the victim had become so exhausted that he could no longer force himself up on the nails, the prolonged asphyxia in the sagging position would quickly bring on death. According to Dr. Barbet, this is what happened to Jesus, who was already severely weakened by the grueling tortures administered before crucifixion.

Barbet's theory had first been tentatively ventured by his predecessor at Saint Joseph's Hospital, Dr. Le Bec, and had later been amplified by Dr. R. W. Hynek, who had witnessed the same types of death—caused by hanging condemned men from a post by their hands, with their feet scarcely touching the ground—inflicted by the Austro-German army. The punishment was called *aufbinden,* and was also used at Dachau.

Barbet found that death by asphyxia was:

borne out by the marks which it has left on the Shroud. We might even say that tetany and asphyxia, of which for a doctor there can be no doubt, prove that the imprints on the Shroud conform with reality; this body died the death of a crucified body.

We can indeed see that the great pectoral muscles, which are the most powerful inspiratory muscles, have been forcibly contracted—they are enlarged, and drawn up toward the collarbone and the arms. The whole thoracic frame is also drawn up, and greatly distended, with a *maximum* inspiration. The epigastric hollow (the pit of the stomach) is sunk and pressed inward, through this elevation and this forward and outward distension of the thorax. . . . The diaphragm, which is a great inspiratory muscle, would also tend to raise the epigastrum in a normal abdominal respiration. With this distension and this forced elevation of the sides, it can only move back toward the abdominal mass; and that is why, above the crossed hands, the hypogastrium, the lower abdomen, can be seen protruding.

Barbet also explained the two directions of the blood flow on the forearms in conjunction with his theory. The long, slender, major flow that runs from the wrist almost to the elbows would have occurred when the body was in the sagging position. The smaller trickles, which can be described as moving toward the ground when the arms were in the almost horizontal position, would have occurred during the times Jesus raised himself to relieve the asphyxia.

Barbet's theory is further supported by the normal method of insuring the rapid death of crucified victims—the breaking of the legs. This method has been verified by historical and archaeological sources, and would have had the effect of preventing the victim from raising himself to ward off the asphyxia. The only plausible reason that such a procedure was not used in the case of Jesus was that he died so rapidly, it was unnecessary. In his case, therefore, the spear thrust in the side was deemed sufficient to legally verify death so that the body could be delivered to Joseph of Arimathaea.

## The Wound in the Heart

According to the Gospel of John, when the soldiers had determined that Jesus was already dead, "one of the soldiers stabbed his side with a lance, and at once there was a flow of blood and water." On the Shroud, on the left side of the rib cage (on the right side of the body because of image reversal), below the armpit is a heavy stain caused by a gaping wound (see Plate 14). This stain, according to medical authorities, is from a combination of blood and clear, organic fluid.

In earlier times it was commonly believed impossible for blood to flow from a corpse and many churchmen had proclaimed the flow of blood and "water" to be a miracle. As a surgeon who had experimented on and dissected numerous cadavers, Barbet knew, to the contrary, that blood does not coagulate in a corpse, but remains liquid for an almost indefinite period, until putrefaction sets in. To him, such a flow was perfectly natural, considering what he had determined about the wound.

In explaining his findings for laymen, Barbet first felt obligated to confront the popular myth that the heart is on the left side. Not so, he said, "the heart is mesial and in front, resting on the diaphragm, between the two lungs. . . . Only its point is definitely to the left, but its base extends to the right beyond the breastbone."

Using the markings of the wound and the bloodstains on the Shroud as his guide, and transferring a duplication of them to the body of a man six feet tall, Barbet hypothesized that the blade of the spear had entered the body above the sixth rib, and had penetrated the pleura (a delicate serous membrane enveloping the lung) and the right lung. Continuing its thrust, the blade then punctured the pericardium (the membranous sac enclosing the heart), and finally pierced the right auricle of the heart (see Plate 15).

In performing experiments on cadavers, Barbet found that blood indeed flowed from the right auricle of the heart, and that the so-far mysterious water was none other than pericardial fluid, or serum, which had accumulated there, only to be released along with the blood at the time the wound was inflicted.

Once again medical science attested to the authenticity of the Shroud, and in this case, also upheld the reality of John's sighting of the blood and "water."

During this phase of his studies, Barbet also found something else:

> On the dorsal image of the Shroud one can see a largish trail at the base of the thorax, stretching the whole way across; on the right side it is fairly broad, and then divides up into little streamlets as it nears the left side of the trunk [See Plate 17]. This trail is caused by a flow of blood. . . . Whence came this blood and why did it flow transversally? Once again, anatomy will give us the reason for this.

131

At the moment of the blow with the lance the dead body was attached to the cross in a vertical position. The right auricle was able to empty itself and probably also the superior vena cava [a large vein in the heart]. . . . But the inferior vena cava [the other large vein in the heart], which lies below it, has remained full. It is long and broad, and we know that when it is cut in an autopsy there is at once a regular flow of blood in the abdomen.

When Joseph of Arimathaea had taken the body down from the cross, he and whoever helped him would have carried the body, *"horizontally,* to the tomb. The blood of the inferior vena cava would then have flowed back into the right auricle and, going through the tunnel made by the lance, which remained gaping open, would have flowed out. But as the body was horizontal, this fresh flow would slip around the right side and would continue to flow transversally *on the back, going right across the lower part of the thorax."*

Could this have been the conception and execution of a fourteenth-century forger?

### The Wounds in the Feet

The wounds in the feet are difficult to study for several reasons. On the frontal image, the knees can be seen clearly, but below them the image becomes gradually less distinct, and the feet virtually invisible. On the dorsal image, the images of the feet are obscured by flows of blood which spread out over the whole length of both feet (see Plate 20). Nonetheless, from the dorsal image it can be determined that the feet were slightly crossed, with the left in front.

From his studies and computations and practical experiments on cadavers, Barbet believed that on the cross the feet were completely crossed, with the left overlapping the right, and with one nail penetrating both and buried into the hard wood of the cross. His experiments showed that if a nail was driven into the feet of a cadaver at the position the wounds appear on the Shroud, the nail would go through a fleshy spot below what is known as Lisfranc's Spaceline, which separates the tarsus from the metatarsals, between the second and third toes (see Plate 21). If the nail were positioned any further toward the tarsus, it would have encountered a mass of bone; any lower and it would probably not have secured the feet to the cross. The images on the Shroud had again corresponded with anatomical reality.

In his conclusion to *A Doctor at Calvary,* Dr. Barbet wrote:

I started out with a certain skepticism . . . to examine the images on the Shroud; I was quite ready to deny their authenticity, if they disagreed with anatomical truth.

But, on the contrary, the facts gradually grouped themselves into a bundle of proofs, which carried increasing conviction. Not only was the explanation of the images so natural and simple that it proclaimed them to be genuine; but, when at first they seemed to be abnormal, experiment demonstrated that they were as they should be, that they could not be different, and as a forger would have portrayed them. . . . Anatomy thus bore witness to their authenticity, in full agreement with the Gospel texts.

The surgeon had performed an autopsy on the Passion and on the Shroud; he pronounced them authentic.

# XI

## *The Evidence of Jehohanan*

When Dr. Barbet conducted his medical studies of the Shroud in the early 1930s, the only knowledge the world had of crucifixion around the time of Jesus came from written records of no great detail, consistency or reliability, and from artistic representations that could by no means be declared historically accurate. Although thousands of men had been crucified during the ancient Roman era, no remains of a crucified victim had ever been found. Such would be the case until 1968.

In June of that year, however, Israeli builders began excavation for an apartment complex at Giv'at ha-Mivtar, about a mile north of the Damascus Gate of the Old City of Jerusalem. Their diggings uncovered three burial caves which housed fifteen limestone ossuaries, all containing human skeletal remains. Of the thirty-five individuals catalogued by anthropologists, five were said to have died by violence. Only one of these concerns us here.

In the ossuary designated I/4 were found the bones of an adult male in his mid-twenties and a child. Outside the tomb were two inscriptions bearing the name, presumably, of the adult male—Jehohanan. Jehohanan met his death by crucifixion.

Of the date of execution, Dr. V. Tzaferis of the Israeli Department of Antiquities and Museums says:

> Mass crucifixions in Judea are mentioned under Alexander Janneus, during the revolt against the census of A.D. 7, and again during the Jewish revolt which brought about the final destruction of the Second Temple in A.D. 70. Individuals were also crucified occasionally by the Roman procurators. Since the pottery and ossuaries found in Tomb I exclude the period of Alexander Janneus for this crucifixion, and since the general situation during the revolt of A.D. 70 excludes the possibility of burial in Tomb I, it would seem that [Jehohanan] was either a rebel put to death at the time of the census revolt in A.D. 7 or the victim of some occasional crucifixion. It is possible, therefore, to place this crucifixion between the start of the first century A.D. and somewhere just before the outbreak of the first Jewish revolt.

Although Jehohanan's remains were in an extremely poor state of preservation, the information they have yielded has been of great significance, both in respect to our knowledge of crucifixions generally and to the continuing effort at authenticating the Shroud. If Dr. Tzaferis' calculations are correct, and if the crucifixion of Jehohanan was typical in method—and there is no indication it was not—then there is at least a reasonable comparison that can be drawn between the crucifixion of Jehohanan and that of Jesus, as evidenced by the markings on the Shroud.

One of the men instrumental in the recovery, reconstruction and study of Jehohanan's remains was Dr. Nicu Haas of the Department of Anatomy, Hebrew University-Hadassah Medical School. Having separated the bones of Jehohanan from those of the child, and satisfied themselves that there was no evidence of a third individual, Dr. Haas and his colleagues found three specific marks of violence on Jehohanan, all relating directly or indirectly to death by crucifixion. There were no other marks of violence or deformations, and it is believed that Jehohanan had been remarkably healthy.

The most important discovery was two calcaneal (heel) bones pierced and joined by a single, large iron nail. Below the head of the nail, between it and the bones, were the remains of a wooden plaque, hewn from *Pistacia* or *Acacia* wood. The purpose of the plaque would have been to further secure the feet to the cross, prohibiting the faint possibility that the victim might be able to tear his feet from the head of the nail. Because of the positioning of the wooden plaque, with the feet between it and the cross, there can be no mistaking it for the footrest, or *suppedaneum,* that was possibly used in some crucifixions. The tip of the nail was bent, and on it were found several small granular-nodular fragments which have been identified as olive wood.

If the crucifixion of Jehohanan had been completed without incident or problem, it is highly unlikely that this unusual artifact—the two heel bones still joined by the nail which anchored them to the cross—would exist. But from all the evidence—the bent nail with its fragments of olive wood and the fact that Jehohanan's feet were amputated after his death—it is believed that the nail struck a knot in the olive wood, thus bending it and making it difficult to remove when it came time to take Jehohanan down from the cross. Rather than attempting to remove the whole body, which under the circumstances would have proved incredibly awkward, the executioners simply amputated the feet and carved out the tough chunk of wood, both still attached to the nail. This was then dumped into the tomb with the rest of Jehohanan's remains.

Although the bones of Jehohanan's left arm were too poorly preserved to be studied with much success, on the right radius (a major bone of the forearm) is evidence of a small scratch that Dr. Haas describes as resembling an incisure that would have been produced on fresh bone by compression and friction. He thus concludes that the scratch was caused by the penetration of a nail between the radius and the ulna (the other major bone of the forearm). Other details of the scratch indicate that the victim must have writhed in anguish toward the end of his ordeal, causing the nail to scrape against the bone.

From severe fractures of the lower leg bones (the tibiae and left fibula), Dr. Haas and his colleagues were able to conclude that Jehohanan received a direct, deliberate blow to that area of his legs. This blow undoubtedly was issued as the *coup de grâce* or *crurifragium* that insured the rapid death of crucified victims.

After a painstaking and complicated study of all aspects of Jehohanan's remains, Dr. Haas was able to describe the position of the body on the cross: "The feet were joined almost parallel, both transfixed by the same nail at the heels, with the legs adjacent; the knees were doubled, the right one overlapping the left; the trunk was contorted; the upper limbs were stretched out, each stabbed by a nail in the forearm."

As it applies to the Shroud and to the crucifixion of Jesus, the evidence of Jehohanan is circumstantial at best. It must also be granted that the crucifixions of Jehohanan and Jesus as analyzed by Drs. Haas and Barbet were marked by some variations. Nonetheless, Jehohanan does provide the only extant conclusive proof of crucifixion methods, and the similarities with Dr. Barbet's findings are obvious.

In both cases, the nails supporting the bodies were not driven through the palms, as has been popularly believed, but through the wrists or forearms, between bones which would have adequately supported the weight of contorted and writhing bodies.

In both cases, only one nail secured both feet to the cross, and while this could not be construed as typical procedure from only two cases, the evidence of each is supportive of the other.

In addition, the *crurifragium* administered to Jehohanan was almost certainly a common practice, and not only lends weight to the Gospel and historical testaments to such, but also makes the reason that Jesus was spared such abuse—he was already dead, so it was unnecessary—much more compelling.

# XII

## *The Other Theories*

It has been frequently stated that if you mention the Shroud to an historian, he will immediately declare it a forgery; but if you show it to a scientist, he will cast his vote for authenticity. Since the beginning of the serious study of the Shroud prompted by Drs. Vignon and Delage, various aspects of it have been dealt with by surgeons, anatomists, forensic scientists, radiologists, chemists, physicians, biologists and pathologists. They are virtually unanimous in their belief that it is authentic, at least insofar as this can be determined prior to sophisticated testing of the actual cloth, which is crucial to conclusive proof. However, while there is agreement on the central issue, there is also, as might well be expected, considerable disagreement about some of the details.

Scientists have debated the cause of death, the origins of the blood and "water" that flowed from the wound in the side, the exact way in which Jesus was enshrouded in the tomb and numerous other issues that bear relevance to the Shroud. In the opinion of this writer, however, the great majority of these disagreements will never be solved to everyone's satisfaction, and the theories already presented in this book currently seem to be the most authoritative and substantial.

There remains one major area of disagreement that is important, and that is the cause of the body images on the Shroud.

## The Vaporograph Theory

Until the end of his life, Paul Vignon remained a devoted partisan to the authenticity of the Shroud, and his second book about it, the monumental *Le Saint Suaire de Turin devant la science, l'archéologie, l'histoire, l'iconographie, la logique,* was published in 1938. Unfortunately it was never published in English translation, even though, while flawed, it is one of the seminal works in the field.

Vignon's vaporograph theory had come under intense criticism, and while he always maintained that it had neither been disproved nor replaced with anything more substantial, he was one of his own sternest critics and would express his reservations. In particular, he pointed out the difficulty of reconciling the notion of a moist cloth clinging to the body as it must have done in order to be stained with the blood and at the same time projecting an image so perfect and so subtle in its detail, that it would seem impossible if the Shroud itself had not been a perfectly flat surface. In addition he recognized, along with several others, that the ammoniacal vapors might not have acted as effectively on the aloes-impregnated cloth as he previously had thought; the amount of urea might not have been sufficient, and its transformation through fermentation might have taken too long.

The vaporograph theory has not, however, been disproved, as Vignon rightfully pointed out. If the images on the Shroud did result from natural causes, they did so because of some kind of chemical reaction. And as anyone who understands basic chemistry knows, even the slightest variance in quantities, timing, temperature or moisture can significantly affect a chemical change. Since there is probably no way that the exact circumstances of what happened in Jesus' tomb can be duplicated—unless new evidence comes to light, the vaporograph theory must stand with the others as a distinct possibility.

## The Direct Contact Theories

Disturbed by the seeming implausibilies of Vignon's theory, two experts in forensic medicine, Dr. Giovanni Judica-Cordiglia and Dr. R. Romanese, and the chemist Dr. P. Scotti, did their own individual tests in an effort to determine the cause of the images.

Dr. Cordiglia moistened a corpse with blood and covered it with a strip of linen soaked in a solution of olive oil and turpentine (certain resinous substances are believed to have been part of the mixture with which the Shroud was anointed) mixed with aloes. When he exposed the linen-draped body to hot steam in the presence of light, he was able to produce images with the negative characteristics, if not nearly the perfection, of those on the Shroud.

Dr. Romanese dampened a corpse with a solution of physiological salt, which is found naturally in any perspiration, and sprinkled linen with powdered aloes. When the linen was draped over the corpse and exposed to light, Romanese was also able to produce crude images similar to those of the Shroud.

Dr. Scotti conducted extensive studies into the

nature of aloes. As we have already learned, an emulsion of aloes in olive oil yields aloetine. Vignon believed that ammoniacal vapors were necessary to react with the aloetine in order for the cloth to brown and thus form images. But Scotti's experiments showed that simple contact with the air could cause the aloetine-soaked cloth to begin to form images. The images are extremely faint at first, but darken with time. In addition, exposure to sunlight makes the images much more pronounced and their color more vivid.

Scotti's findings have particular appeal for those who have always been bothered by John's failure to mention the images when he found the burial clothes in Jesus' tomb. If Scotti's theory is correct, they say, the images had not yet formed, and did not form until sometime later. Adhering to Scotti's theory, it is reasonable to assume that images might have taken some months to form, thus providing justification for John's silence. But it stretches the imagination to believe that such a process could have taken centuries, which some scholars have ventured as the reason that early claimants to having seen the Shroud did not discern the images.

At any rate, the images produced by Cordiglia, Romanese and Scotti are only slightly more realistic than those produced by Vignon, and so their theories remain no more than that, none of them being fully acceptable.

All of these theories do, however, point to the necessity of the Shroud having been anointed with some kind of aromatic that facilitated a chemical reaction. In this common ground, they are somewhat supported by a find made in Antinoe, Egypt. Antinoe was a town built on the Nile by the Roman emperor Hadrian in A.D. 132. Between the years 1897 and 1902, Albert Gayet unearthed in the excavations at Antinoe approximately ten thousand bodies, some of which were pagan and some Christian, in an intact state. Some of the Christian bodies had undergone shroud burials, and according to the Reverend Maurus Green, Gayet found "one case of a face veil, folded in four, that bears the apparently undistorted imprint of the dead person's face, similar to the Shroud's death mask. The experts think that this fourfold impression was made by some chemical process involving spices."

The Reverend Peter Rinaldi and others hold that the vaporograph and direct contact theories "are not mutually exclusive," and that more experimentation and more careful research on the Shroud itself may well prove that there are valid elements in both theories.

## The Scorch-Picture Theory

Throughout this book, we have so far explored the Shroud within the bounds of natural laws, scientifically acceptable premises and accountable phenomena. In remaining within these limits, we have dealt with Jesus only as a historical personage and have cautiously accepted the Gospel accounts of the Passion as being basically factual. Such explanations should be acceptable to Jew or Christian, atheist or agnostic. But we have also found that neither the vaporograph nor the direct contact theories offer completely acceptable explanations of the causation of the body images on the Shroud, at least based on the evidence to date. It is here that we must confront the possibility of Jesus' resurrection, and what effect it might have had on the Shroud.

In 1966, bothered that none of the prevailing explanations for the causation of the body images seemed definitive, Geoffrey Ashe, a British scholar, began experimenting with the production of images on linen through heat radiation. Using a heated brass ornament on which there was a horse in relief, he found that by placing linen over it, a clear negative image could be formed by a combination of direct contact and heat radiation. The results were far more impressive in their affinity to the images on the Shroud than those produced by any of the other experiments.

Writing in *Sindon,* a periodical devoted exclusively to research into the Shroud and distributed selectively to sindonologists throughout the world, Ashe said:

> The Shroud is explicable if it once enwrapped a human body to which something extraordinary happened. It is not explicable otherwise. The Christian Creed has always affirmed that Our Lord underwent an unparalleled transformation in the tomb. His case is exceptional and perhaps here is the key. It is at least intelligible (and has been suggested several times) that the physical change of the body at the Resurrection may have released a brief and violent burst of some other radiation than heat, perhaps scientifically identifiable, perhaps not, which scorched the cloth. In this case the Shroud image is a quasi photograph of Christ returning to life, produced by a kind of radiance or "incandescence" partially analogous to heat in its effects .... Also, the fact that the bloodstains on the Shroud are positive is now readily accounted for. The

145

blood was matter which had ceased to be part of the body, underwent no change at the Resurrection, and therefore did not scorch, but marked the cloth differently.

Dr. David Willis, a British physician and noted sindonologist, has said of the Ashe theory:

Perhaps, in our present state of knowledge, that is as good an explanation as any. It is consistent with the present conception of matter as forms of energy and the fact of radiation images formed on stone following the dropping of the atomic bomb at Hiroshima. It also ties in with Leo Vala's conviction that the Shroud image is in some way "photographic." Vala is a brilliant, inventive photographer. As an agnostic his conviction is impressive: "I can prove conclusively that claims calling the Shroud a fake are completely untrue. Even with today's highly advanced photographic resources nobody alive could produce the image—a photographic negative—embodied in the Shroud."

As can be determined from his reserved tone, Geoffrey Ashe is neither a religious hysteric nor a fool. He is a Christian, and any immediate acceptance of his proposal, whether it will ever actually be provable or not, requires an unwavering belief in the Resurrection as an absolute fact. It also defines the Shroud as having been subject to supernatural intervention—a miracle. For some people such faith is an integral part of their religious lives, and to them, Ashe's theory may be the most palatable of all, correlating as it does the Resurrection with the remarkable picture that endures.

But what of the atheist and the agnostic, who,

while accepting the historicity of Jesus, reject the notion of resurrection as but another apocryphal story, put forth by the disciples to further the spread of Christianity? Must they also dismiss the possibility of radiation-caused images out-of-hand?

Possibly not, for recent experiments with psychics and "healers" seem to indicate that these people are capable of emitting some kind of energy, which may be either the cause or effect of whatever extraordinary faculties they may possess. No evidence so far indicates that this energy could be capable of producing anything like the images on the Shroud. But if there is any validity to the experiments, we may have to at least consider the idea of energy discharge —resurrection or no—as a possible cause of the images on the Shroud.

However the images were formed, we must understand that at this point we are not so much dealing with the actual cause as with individual perceptions of it, based largely on speculative experiments rather than direct evidence. A complete and thorough physical testing of the Shroud may reveal enough clues so that a satisfactory conclusion may be set forth in the future. But until then, no plausible theory can be completely dismissed, and even the most far-fetched must be considered. As Geoffrey Ashe so eloquently and simply put it, "The Shroud is explicable if it once enwrapped a human body to which something extraordinary happened. It is not explicable otherwise."

# XIII

## Can the Shroud Perform Miracles?

The subject of miracles is a highly controversial one, about which most people have opinions, though none have any satisfactory answers. There are certainly those who accept religious miracles just as they accept the supernatural concept of God. Providing much substance, if no proof, to claims of religious miracles are the numerous nonmedically induced cures of physical ailments catalogued at the Roman Catholic shrine of Lourdes in France.

However, there seems to be a popular misconception that relics or shrines *cause* miracles. Strictly speaking, this is not true. According to the doctrine of the Catholic Church, miracles are caused by supernatural intervention to relieve the suffering of the faithful. God's all-powerful benevolence and the faith of the recipient of a miracle are the essential elements, and relics and shrines are only material symbols through which believers express their faith and offer up their prayers.

Medical doctors have studied the aspects of "faith healing," whether through relics or shrines or through the activities of the so-called healers, who are becoming more and more prominent and attracting increasing scientific interest. Some cases, of course, fall apart as hoaxes; others reflect radical, if only temporary, remission; while still others indicate genuine cures. Some contemporary psychologists translate the "faith" of the recipients of cures into a kind of psychosomatic effect; that is, the emotional condition of the person is in fact responsible for the physical change, and while the person may well believe that his cure is the result of supernatural intervention, he has, in effect, cured himself.

But what of the documented and controlled experiments in which such healers have had a positive or curative effect on plants, enzymes and rats? Can these nonhuman subjects also be affected by internal psychosomatics, or are the changes in them produced by some as yet undefinable energy flow from the healers? At our present state of knowledge, although both skeptics and believers will scoff at such reserve, it would seem premature either to reject miracles as such, or to accept them. We simply know too little about ourselves or about the forces that affect us to come to hard and fast conclusions.

We do know that throughout the documented history of the Shroud, there are a few vague references to miracles attributed to it, but there is so little substance to these stories that any conclusions about them are impossible. In 1692, for instance, it was believed that Turin was spared from the Black Plague as a result of direct appeals to the Shroud. A bronze plaque on a Turin city wall commemorates this "miracle." Obviously, the plague could have avoided Turin's residents for any number of natural, accountable reasons, and there is no way any direct correlation that would involve miracles can be ventured at this time.

It does seem odd that such an unusual relic of the church, venerated by so many millions of pilgrims during the limited expositions held throughout its history, is not the subject of countless stories of great wonders attributed to it, whether factual or apocryphal. But it is not, and one can only speculate that its inaccessibility, even during the expositions, provided a dampening effect on rumors, and that the reserve with which the church has treated it further chilled the outgrowth of such stories.

The only documented modern account of a miraculous cure being sought directly through the Shroud occurred in 1955. During the Second World War, British Royal Air Force Captain G. L. Cheshire had been a much-decorated war hero. After the war, the publication of his best-selling memoirs, *Bomber Pilot,* made him a national celebrity. A convert to Catholicism, he then devoted his life to philanthropic work. Owing to his fame and his well-publicized efforts at helping people, on May 11, 1955, he received the following letter:

Gloucester, May 10

Dear Mr. Cheshire:

I am writing to ask you if my daughter Josephine could be blessed with the relic of the Holy Shroud. Josephine is ten years old and she is very ill in hospital—with osteomylitis in the hip and leg. Also a lung abscess. Her doctor has told me that there is no hope of Josephine getting better. She has been in and out of hospital for the last five years. On Friday she received the last rites of Holy Church. Josephine has asked me to write to you and she said if only she could see the relic she will get better and walk again. Everyone at the hospital has been very good to her. She is always in great pain but she has always got a smile . . .

I know I am asking for great things, but I do hope and pray that my prayers will be answered for my daughter to get better.

I remain,

Mrs. Veronica Woollam

Cheshire was away when the letter arrived, so an assistant in his office answered Mrs. Woollam, saying that the Shroud was in Turin, and that it was not shown to the public except during rare expositions. The assistant also enclosed a photograph of the face on the Shroud.

Upon his return home, Cheshire was sympathetic to the young girl's plea, but believed he could do nothing. Five days later, however, he received another letter from Josephine's mother, this one telling him that the girl was no longer on her death bed, but up and around the hospital ward in a wheelchair. As Cheshire put it, "Someone talked hopefully of a miracle, but this we stopped, pointing out that we had nothing concrete to go on and that in any case for a cure to be recognized as miraculous it must, among other requirements, be complete and permanent. Josie's cure could not be complete, for she was still in hospital."

Two weeks later, "a third letter arrived. Josie had been discharged and was back at home. Moreover, for the first time there was a note of joy—almost of triumph."

On June 17, Cheshire visited the Woollam home without warning. Josie was in her wheelchair and showed him her legs. They were deformed and mutilated, but before the arrival of the photograph of the Shroud they had also been open and running. The receipt of the photograph had coincided with the remarkable remission of the disease.

Although skeptical that actually seeing or touching the Shroud could help the girl fully recover and walk again, Cheshire was astounded at her recovery at that point, and resolved to do everything he could to help.

In July, Cheshire and Josie journeyed to Turin, stopping on the way to get permission from Humbert II for Josie to see and hold the Shroud. While countless other requests had gone unheeded over the years, every effort was made to accommodate Josie. When they arrived in Turin, the king had already telephoned ahead, authorizing the authorities of the archdiocese to grant any reasonable request Josie might make.

A special mass was said on her behalf and she was allowed to see and hold the Shroud on her lap. There was no miracle; there was no cure. There was, however, a radiant young crippled girl who understood that while she would remain afflicted, she had also done something that few people would ever do—she had touched the Holy Shroud.

It is saddening that Josie was not blessed with a miracle, or with a cure by any means; but those who may be disappointed that there is just no evidence of miracles related to the Shroud should be cognizant of the attitude of some of the Shroud's most dedicated proponents. Is it not enough, they ask, that the Shroud exists at all? For if it is authentic, then it is in and of itself the most miraculous of all miracles— a self-portrait of Jesus Christ.

# XIV

## *The Current State of Affairs*

It is virtually impossible for the intelligent, inquisitive person, no matter what his religious beliefs, to understand the attitude of the Shroud's keepers. As has already been stated, the Shroud is the private property of Humbert II, the head of the House of Savoy and the exiled king of Italy. It is under the care and protection of the Archdiocese of Turin, presided over by Michele Cardinal Pellegrino. Theoretically, Humbert can do anything he wishes with the Shroud—leave it where it is, sell it, even destroy it. He is, of course, consulted on any matter that might affect it, but realistically, Cardinal Pellegrino and his delegate for Shroud affairs, Monsignor Cottino, have almost absolute control.

Until 1969, despite constant pleading from responsible men of science and of the church for more study, for direct scientific testing of the actual cloth, for the public to have greater access, for any sign of interest or movement from the powers that be, it was almost as if the Shroud did not exist. Locked in its silver casket, sealed and constantly guarded, it was there in Turin as it had been since 1578, but it had been unseen and untouched since the exposition of 1933. The faithful worshiped in the cathedral; pilgrims visited the Shroud museum in the archdiocese complex; books and articles were written about the Shroud. But inquiries about or petitions for further study were either ignored or put off with evasive, ambiguous replies.

Over the years, many questions have been asked about this intransigent attitude. Is the church afraid that the Shroud is a fake? Does the church know it is a fake? Are the authorities fearful that it might be destroyed or damaged?

If the Shroud is authentic, then it is the greatest relic known to Christianity; why, then, are Christians not allowed to see it?

The answers are not forthcoming. John Walsh says:

> For some, this attitude is incomprehensible at best, and at worst it points to a fear of what might be disclosed. The truth is, however, that this problem of physical testing is not a simple one. The Shroud is, after all, a spiritual object, hallowed by the prayers and devotions of many millions of pilgrims, and by the veneration of Popes and saints. Its true value is religious and, if authentic, it goes far beyond even such archaeological wonders as the Rosetta Stone or the clay tablets of Nineveh. Those who have inherited the task of safeguarding it and preserving it into the future feel their obligation heavily. They are understandably slow to endanger even the smallest fragment of it.

The Reverend Peter M. Rinaldi is not nearly so charitable, but then he has spent the greatest part of his adult life in frustrating efforts to obtain complete authentication of the Shroud and to publicize it as much as possible. Rinaldi first saw the Shroud as an altar boy in the Cathedral of Turin during the exposition of 1933. For the past twenty-odd years he has been pastor of the Corpus Christi Church in Port Chester, New York. Adjacent to the church, he has erected a magnificent shrine to "the Christ of the Holy Shroud," which features a life-sized illuminated reproduction of the Shroud. Rinaldi is also one of the moving forces in the Holy Shroud Guild, an international, loosely knit group of scholars, scientists and clergymen whose efforts are devoted to further study of the Shroud and its eventual authentication.

Commenting on Walsh's explanation for the attitude of the Turin officials, Rinaldi says, "These remarks are both well-reasoned and kind, but they hardly justify the 'iron curtain of silence' some responsible authorities have clamped down on the Shroud. Among these authorities the jealous or timid custodians of the Shroud's citadel in Turin are unquestionably the ones who, for reasons best known to themselves, have consistently delayed the progress of the Shroud's cause."

Rinaldi is an erudite, gentle man. He is also probably the single most knowledgeable man in the world, and certainly in the United States, about all aspects of the Shroud. In numerous conversations with him, I have never heard him raise his voice in anger against the intransigence of the Turin authorities. It is raised in frustration, for Rinaldi himself cannot understand. And while whatever slight progress had been made is largely the result of the efforts of the Fathers Rinaldi and Otterbein, the dedication on the part of the Turin authorities is still not equal to the subject. True, Cardinal Pellegrino is not a well man; true, the Turin archdiocese has problems other than those concerning the Shroud;

true, the Shroud is the subject of considerable political pressure from many viewpoints; but none of these problems can conceivably warrant what Rinaldi humorously refers to as "the scandal of the Shroud."

In June of 1969, something finally happened. A small, secret panel of experts—in archaeology, chemistry, physiology and medicine—was allowed to spend three days examining the Shroud. Although he had been archbishop of Turin for a number of years, Cardinal Pellegrino then saw the Shroud for the first time, and that fact alone is indicative of the lack of concern with which he had previously treated the cloth. That the secret study had taken place at all might never have been made public had it not been for a leak to a strange man who calls himself Kurt Berna or John Reban. His real name is Hans Naber, and his involvement with the Shroud provides one of the most bizarre episodes in its history. Surprisingly, the usual garden-variety eccentrics and charlatans who seem to have a special talent for attaching themselves to the unusual and mysterious have stayed away from the Shroud—with the single exception of Hans Naber.

Some years ago, Naber latched onto the issue of the Shroud. The basis for his interest seems to have stemmed from some kind of visions which he claimed demonstrated to him that Jesus did not die on the cross. He further claimed that the markings on the Shroud proved this. In 1967, Naber—writing under the name John Reban—published a book entitled *Inquest on Jesus Christ,* in which he expounded his theories, and which sold briskly in England and in Europe. In the book, his own "studies" were buttressed with the testimony of numerous "scientific experts" who wished to remain anonymous in order to protect their objectivity.

In fact, the experts remained anonymous because they were nonexistent. Virtually every word that Naber has ever uttered or written on the subject of the Shroud has been thoroughly discredited by the investigations of Professor Werner Bulst and Dr. David Willis, and it is just unfortunate that so many unsuspecting readers, apparently including Naber's English publisher, were taken in.

In 1970, Naber was arrested on charges of fraud in a matter unrelated to the Shroud. That arrest came too late, however, to stop him from making one last round of headlines with his ridiculous charges. Learning of the secret examination conducted in 1969, Naber used the world press to denounce it as an attempt on the part of the Catholic Church to destroy the Shroud, his "evidence" that Jesus did not die on the cross.

As absurd as Naber's claims were, they did force the Turin authorities into an awkward and embarrassing position. Yet instead of being completely forthcoming and candid, Cardinal Pellegrino issued only the briefest of statements about the secret study. It had been conducted, he said, merely to determine the condition of the Shroud, and to ascertain whether any measures were necessary to protect the cloth against deterioration or damage from Turin's industrial smog. The names of the experts involved were not revealed, "in order to shield them from the kind of publicity that would rather hinder than favor their researches," and to this day the written reports they filed have not been made public.

Although no responsible critic would place the

activities of the Turin authorities on the same level as Naber's, their secrecy does ironically fall to some degree into the same pattern. The reports have been so guarded that months after the study had been conducted, Humbert complained to Father Rinaldi that he had only seen one of them, and that one only because the expert in question was a personal friend of his.

The results of the still-secret study again raise the question of whether the authorities know or have any reason to believe at this point that the Shroud is a fake. If anything is true, it is probably the opposite; that is, if the secret study concerned itself with the issue of authenticity at all, then to whatever extent it did so, the evidence continued to be supportive of authenticity. There are several solid, if not absolutely concrete, reasons for this opinion.

Regardless of the secrecy surrounding the 1969 study, it is almost certain that one of the experts who participated was Dr. Giovanni Judica-Cordiglia, a proponent of the direct-contact theory, former professor of forensic medicine at the University of Milan and now director of the International Center of Holy Shroud Studies in Turin. Dr. Cordiglia's medical studies of the Shroud have gone on for years, and his observations and conclusions have in many ways equaled Barbet's. Although whatever report he may have prepared in 1969 remains secret, Dr. Cordiglia still believes wholeheartedly in the authenticity of the Shroud and maintains that, based on legally acceptable medical evidence, the Shroud could be so judged in a court of law. If there were any data contradicting these opinions, certainly a man of Cordiglia's stature would not continue to maintain them.

Another reason for maintaining faith in the legitimacy of the Shroud is the remarkable statement (partially reproduced later) issued by Pope Paul VI, on videotape, on the occasion of the televised exposition of the Shroud in November 1973. Although it is general and somewhat guarded in tone, it is inconceivable that the Pope would have made such a statement if any recent evidence had pointed to forgery.

Following his own personal observation of the Shroud during the 1969 study, Cardinal Pellegrino's attitude changed, if not for the best, then at least for the better. Preparations began for some kind of public exposition of the cloth, and the cardinal seemed more receptive to proposals for actual physical tests.

On Friday evening, November 23, 1973, the Shroud was the subject of a televised exposition which was broadcast throughout most of Europe and parts of South America. The date had been set and postponed several times, and long and agonizing conferences hammered out the details, which changed frequently and abruptly. Months before the exposition was to take place, this writer requested permission to be present, along with other members of the press, concerned scholars, clergy and scientists. I volunteered to obey any strictures that might be placed on my presence. I wanted, indeed I needed, to see the mysterious ancient cloth that had for so long occupied my time and my thoughts. In spite of the efforts of Father Rinaldi, who made every effort on my behalf, I was told that no outsiders would be allowed access to the Shroud; that there would be no press conference; and that no one would be admitted to the cathedral when the cloth was displayed other than the television crew and Turin officials. I was thus faced with an expensive and frustrating journey, only to sit in a hotel room and see the Shroud on Italian television. I decided not to go.

A similar experience was had by George Suski and Mort Fallick, respectively the American producer and director who are working on a comprehensive television documentary on the Shroud. For this documentary, Suski and Fallick had already spent many thousands of dollars, shot on location throughout the world and amassed thousands of feet of film. An opportunity for them to film the exposition would have provided a fitting climax to their work. They were told not only were they unwelcome, but that if they attempted to bring their film crew the Italian crew would walk off, thus possibly interrupting the exposition. They, too, decided to stay home.

As it turned out, however, a press conference was held prior to the exposition, and a number of people were allowed to see the Shroud at close range, and to photograph it.

I have not recounted the above stories out of anger. We were disappointed, certainly, and to some extent our work on the Shroud was hindered, but our experiences are really nothing more than fresh examples of how haphazardly affairs relating to the Shroud have been handled.

During the press conference Cardinal Pellegrino explained why the exposition was to be televised, rather than held in public:

The medium of television is a modern and up-to-date technique which makes it possible for millions of people to contemplate the precious relic at the same time. So high a number of spectators could not have been attained at a traditional exposition, which would have involved, among other things, many problems of organization and logistics, and which would have subjected the Shroud to the risk of wear and to the action of substances in the atmosphere. Many people, moreover, would not have been able to come to Turin. Those, especially, who need the comfort of this document of the passion of Jesus—the poor, the aged, the infirm—would not have had an opportunity to see it.

Cardinal Pellegrino also stressed the religious aspects of the presentation:

The significance and value of the relic are so great as to overcome every legitimate doubt. It must be distinguished from the disputed question of the authenticity of the Holy Shroud. It is a reminder, a most effective reminder, of Him whom all humanity, believing and unbelieving, regards with veneration. It has something to say to everyone. . . .

The exposition, estimated to have reached as many as 200 million people, consisted of six parts: an introduction by the writer Fortunato Pasqualino; a videotape of the message of Pope Paul VI; a videotape of the Shroud being removed from the reliquary; an illustrated history of the Shroud; general and detailed views of the Shroud, including positive and negative images of the face; and an address by Cardinal Pellegrino.

Among his remarks, Pope Paul said:

161

# THE FIFTH GOSPEL

To our venerable brother Michele Cardinal Pellegrino, Archbishop of Turin, and to all of the holy and beloved Church entrusted to his pastoral ministry and in full communion with us. And to all who are, by means of radio and television, following this ceremony.

We, too, as though we were present, fix the gaze of our spirit, in most attentive and devoted admiration, on the sacred Shroud, of which a pious and extraordinary exposition has been arranged at Turin, the custodian of this singular treasure.

We know how much research is concentrated on the celebrated relic, and we are not unaware of how much fervent and heartfelt piety surrounds it. We personally still remember the vivid impression that was stamped upon our spirit when, in May 1931, we had the good fortune to be present, on the occasion of special observances then being rendered to the Shroud, at a projection of it upon a large lighted screen; and the face of Christ, there represented, seemed to us more true, more profound, more human and divine, than any other image we had been able to admire and to venerate. This was, for us, a moment of extraordinary enchantment.

Whatever scientific and historical judgment competent scholars may pass on this astonishing and mysterious relic, we cannot refrain from praying that it may not only bring those who examine it to an intense physical examination of the exterior and mortal lineaments of the Savior, but bring them also to a more penetrating vision of His fascinating mystery. . . .

What good fortune, then, and what a mystery to see Jesus! Him, Jesus Himself! Is that beatitude denied to us, remote as we are in time and space? How can we, too, gaze upon that human face, splendid in Him as Son of Man and Son of God?

162

Perhaps we are like the disciples on their way to Emmaus, whose eyes were clouded and who failed to recognize the resurrected Jesus in the pilgrim who was accompanying them. Or perhaps we must resign ourselves, in accordance with the tradition attested by, for example, Saint Irenaeus and Saint Augustine, to confessing that the mortal appearance of Jesus is completely unknown to us. Great, then, is our good fortune if the effigy which is alleged to survive on the sacred Shroud permits us to contemplate some of the genuine features of the adorable physical appearance of Our Lord Jesus Christ, and if in truth it offers relief to our avidity, so strong today, for visual knowledge of Him!

As we gather around so precious and pious a relic, His mysterious fascination will grow in all of us, believers and unbelievers alike, and in our hearts will resound the evangelical admonition of His voice, which invites us to seek Him where He still is hidden and still can be found, loved and served in human form. . . .

Since the attitude of the church, as expressed through the pope, is of some consequence, it is important here to compare Pope Paul's statement with the attitudes of some of his predecessors. Writing in *Esquire* magazine in 1971, Karl E. Meyer outlined some of the most significant:

In 1582, Gregory XIII granted a plenary indulgence to all who visited the Shroud when it was exposed in that year; in 1814, when he was returning from the Coronation of Napoleon, and again a year later, when he passed through Turin, Pius VII prostrated himself before the Shroud, and solemnly incensed the relic; new indulgences were granted on successive exhibitions by Gregory XVI, Pius IX and

Leo XIII; Pius X enriched the devotion which was attached to the image of the Shroud after 1898; and in 1936, Pius XI, who had scientific training and who took a special interest in the Shroud, gave photographs of the fabric to a group of Catholic Action pilgrims, and spoke these words: "These are pictures which divine Providence has sent precisely for you. . . . They are pictures that come to us from the Holy Shroud of Turin, which is still an object of mystery, but which certainly was not made by human hands, as can now be said to be demonstrated." More recently, John XXIII, after looking at the Shroud's image, was heard to say, "This can only be the Lord's doing!"

By either act or utterance, over thirty popes have contributed to the belief in the Shroud's authenticity, although it should be noted that, in the words of Father Rinaldi:

Its authenticity, like the authenticity of any relic, is not within the scope of the Church's doctrinal definitions. She leaves it to archaeology and other related sciences. A well-established tradition is all the Church requires to permit the cult of a relic. Unless science can clearly disprove a relic's claim to authenticity, the Church will not interfere. We should remember, too, that (as in the case of images and statues) the cult or veneration is directly intended for the person of Christ or of a given saint, and only indirectly for the relic itself.

As the televised exposition of 1973 closed, Cardinal Pellegrino said:

Let us present ourselves before the dead and living Christ, now and forever, with all the weight of our sufferings, and the sufferings of the poor, the oppressed, the infirm, the underprivileged, in whom the image of Christ is even more vividly reflected: for if it can be doubted, as some do doubt, that the image we piously venerate is really the imprint left by the body of Christ on the new shroud in which it was wrapped by Joseph of Arimathaea, one thing is beyond doubt, and that is that the face of Christ is imprinted in that of his brothers and ours, of those who have, for all too many selfish and indifferent people, neither faces nor voices. May this hour of intense emotion not pass in vain; may it leave in our spirits an ineradicable imprint of generous acceptance of the Cross and of effective solidarity with our brothers.

If the televised exposition was almost solely religious in nature, and took great pains to ignore the question of authenticity or further testing, then that is all that could be expected—for the moment. That the first exposition of the Shroud in forty years was held at all is at least indicative of some movement on the part of the Turin authorities, and they have promised that the tests will go forward. They must, and with all due speed, because the issue of the Shroud's authenticity just will not go away. It can only become more controversial if the proper steps are postponed much longer.

Throughout this book, and in anything else one hears or reads about the Shroud, the matter of direct, physical, scientific testing of the cloth is the predominant concern. Indirect study has gone as far as it can go, and every indication favors authenticity. It may be that, no matter which tests are applied, there will never be a completely conclusive determination of authenticity; but the issue can only be resolved if every conceivable effort is made.

It is impossible at this point to say what further tests can show until after they are done, for there are so many unknown factors to be taken into account. For instance, it is possible that at one point during the early history of the Shroud, it was boiled in oil in a bizarre effort to see if the images could be removed. Most scholars doubt that this episode actually ever took place, and there is certainly no visible indication of it remaining, but if it did, the effects of the oil could contaminate some of the chemical tests. And that early history is so obscure and fragmented, who knows to what other strange tortures the Shroud was subject?

For years, the possibility of carbon-14 dating was proposed as the most likely way of determining the age of the cloth. But regardless of the present controversy that surrounds this method and the possibility that it would not yield satisfactory results when applied to the Shroud, it is virtually certain that it will never be used because of the necessity of destroying a part of the Shroud in the process. And no one, not even the most vociferous proponents of further tests, is willing to risk that.

Spectroscopy, or spectrum analysis, might be able to determine whether the bloodstains are real, from a human being, and possibly even type them.

Microscopic studies of the body images or direct chemical analysis of them may reveal more definitive conclusions as to their cause.

A NASA scientist at Houston's Space Center has ventured the possibility that the computerized technique used to enhance photographs beamed back from space probes might be able to do the same with the "photograph" on the Shroud, thus giving a clearer picture and a better sense of detail. A group in England has proposed trying the same chemical process which was recently responsible for experts being able to declare the famed Vinland Map a fake.

Color and infrared photographs have already been taken, but these were disappointing from the standpoint of any new revelations. Black-and-white photographs are still the most revealing.

During the time they were able to observe the cloth at close range in November 1973, both Father Rinaldi and Dr. David Willis were struck by the comparison between the appearance of the body images and the scorch marks left by the Chambéry fire. They seem to have the same visual properties, and should chemical analysis of the images yield no further proof of natural causation, then a microscopic comparison might lend further credence to the possibilities of radiation as the cause.

There are also numerous other possibilities for tests which might or might not provide interesting results. At this point, however, the concern is not so much with what can be determined, but that the tests move forward rapidly. Certainly no one wishes even the smallest part of the Shroud to be damaged, but scientific sophistication is presently such that a series of perfectly safe tests may yield sufficient results as to make any damage unnecessary.

# XV

## *Conclusion*

There is not currently a satisfactory conclusion to the story of the Shroud of Turin. There can be none until the scientific testing of the cloth has been completed; and although the results of those tests are being awaited with great optimism, they may not be sufficient to categorically certify or deny authenticity. Nonetheless, the weight of evidence already at hand is remarkably impressive, and even the most skeptical no longer rush to the attack, but maintain relative silence. Some arguments do continue, but basically these are restricted to rather esoteric points which, while not unimportant, will not significantly affect the final judgment.

But even if the tests prove the Shroud is not a fraud, even if it can be conclusively shown that the images of the body were not put there by human hands, even if the bloodstains are genuine, there will be reasonable men who will swear that there is still no way to prove that the imprint of the man on the Shroud is of Jesus. Their point is valid, but in the recorded history of the world, only one man has ever been subjected to the unique combination of tortures proclaimed by the Gospels and evident on the Shroud. That man was Jesus Christ. And, in the end, the ancient cloth of Turin may have to be accepted with the same faith on which the whole of Christianity is based.

# Bibliography

Arndt, W. F., and Gingrich, F. Wilbur. *A Greek–English Lexicon of the New Testament and Other Early Christian Literature.* Cambridge, 1952.

Ashe, Geoffrey. "What Sort of Picture?" *Sindon* (1966): 15–19.

Barbet, Pierre. *A Doctor at Calvary.* Translated by the Earl of Wicklow. New York, 1953.

Barnes, Arthur S. *The Holy Shroud of Turin.* London, 1934.

Bender, A. P. "Beliefs, Rites and Customs of the Jews Connected with Death, Burial and Mourning." *Jewish Quarterly Review* 7 (1894–1895), Pt. 4: 101–18; Pt. 5: 254–69.

Buchler, A. "L'enterrement des criminels d'après le Talmud et le Midrasch." *Revue des Etudes Juives* 46 (1903): 74–88.

Bulst, Werner. *The Shroud of Turin.* Translated by S. McKenna and J. J. Galvin. Milwaukee, 1957.

*Catholic Encyclopaedia.* New York, 1912, S.v. "Shroud, The Holy."

Chevalier, U. *Autour des origines du suaire de Lirey. Avec documents inédits.* Paris, 1903.

*Etude critique sur l'origine du St. Suaire de Lirey-Chambéry-Turin.* Paris, 1900.

*Le St. Suaire de Lirey-Chambéry-Turin et les défenseurs son authenticité.* Paris, 1902.

"Le Saint Suaire de Turin est-il l'original ou une

copie? Etude critique." *Mémoires et documents publiés par la Société savoisienne d'histoire et d'archéologie,* 2nd ser. 13 (1899): 105–33.

"Le saint-suaire de Turin et le nouveau testament." *Revue Biblique* 11 (1902): 564–73.

Chifflet, J. J. *De linteis sepulchralibus Christi crisis historica.* Antwerp, 1624.

Daremberg, C., and Saglio, E., eds. *Dictionnaire des Antiquités.* Paris, 1896. S.vv. "Crux" and "Flagellum."

De Clari, Robert. *La conquête de Constantinople.* Edited by P. Lauer. Paris, 1924.

Delage, Yves. "Le linceul de Turin." *Revue Scientifique* 17 (1902): 683–87.

*Enciclopedia Cattolica.* Vatican City, 1948.

*Encyclopaedia Judaica.* Jerusalem, 1971. S.v. "Burial."

Enrie, Giuseppe. *La Santa Sindone rivelata dalla fotografia.* Turin, 1938.

Epstein, I., ed. *The Babylonian Talmud.* London, 1935–52.

Fossati, L. *Conversazioni e discussioni sulla santa sindone.* Turin, 1968.

*La Santa sindone: nuova luce su antichi documenti.* Turin, 1961.

Geyer, Paulus, ed. *Itinera Hierosolymitana saeculi,* vols. 3–8. Prague, Vienna, Leipzig, 1878.

Graffin, R., and Nau, F., eds. *Patrologia Orientalis.* Paris, 1904–.

Green, Maurus. "Enshrouded in Silence." *Ampleforth Journal* 74 (1969): 319–45.

Haas, N. "Anthropological Observations on the Skeletal Remains from Giv'at ha-Mivtar." *Israel Exploration Journal* 20 (1970): 38–59.

Holzmeister, U. "Crux Domini eiusque crucifixio ex archaeologia romana illustrantur." *Verbum Domini* 14 (1934): 149–55, 216–20, 241–49, 257–63.

*The Interpreter's Dictionary of the Bible.* New York and

Nashville, 1962. S.vv. "Bier, Burial, Embalming, Spice."

*The Jewish Encyclopaedia.* New York and London, 1902.

Judica-Cordiglia, G. "La sepoltura di Gesù e la sacra sindone." *Salesianum* 16 (1954): 153–67.

Klauser, T., ed. *Reallexikon fuer Antike und Christentum.* Stuttgart, 1950–. S.vv. "Christusbild" and "Acheiropoieta."

Meyer, Karl E., "Were You There When They Photographed My Lord?" *Esquire,* August 1971.

Michelant, H., and Raynaut, G., eds. *Itinéraires à Jérusalem.* Geneva, 1882.

Migne, J. L., ed. *Patrologiae Cursus Completus. Series Graeca.* Paris, 1857–66.
*Patrologiae Cursus Completus. Series Latina.* Paris, 1844–64.

Mommsen, T. *Roemisches Strafrecht.* Leipzig, 1899.

Moulton, J. H., and Milligan, G. *The Vocabulary of the Greek New Testament Illustrated from the Papyri and Other Non-Literary Sources.* London, 1942.

Naveh, J. "The Ossuary Inscriptions from Giv'at ha-Mivtar." *Israel Exploration Journal* 20 (1970): 33–37.

*The New Catholic Encyclopedia.* New York, 1967.

*The New English Bible.* New York, 1971.

Pauly, A.; Wissowa, G.; and Kroll, W.; eds. *Real-Encyclopaedie der klassischen Altertumswissenschaft.* Stuttgart, 1893–. S.v. "Crux" by R. Hitzig.

Riant, P. *Des dépouilles religieuses enlevées à Constantinople au XIIIe siècle par les Latins.* Paris, 1875. Extrait des Mémoires de la Société nationale des Antiquaires de France, vol. 36.

Riant, P., ed. *Alexii I Comneni ad Robertum Flandrensem Epistola Spuria.* Geneva, 1877.
*Exuviae Sacrae Constantinopolitanae,* vols. 1 and 2. Geneva, 1877–78.

Ricci, G. *La morte di Cristo contestata in nome della santa sindone*. Assisi, 1970.

*L'uomo della sindone e Gesù*. Rome, 1969.

*Statura dell'uomo della sindone*. Assisi, 1957.

Rinaldi, Peter M. *It Is the Lord*. New York, 1972.

Roberts, C. H., and Turner, E. G., eds. *Catalogue of the Greek Papyri in the John Rylands Library, Manchester*, vol 4. Manchester, 1952.

Savio, P. "Ricerche sopra la santa sindone." *Salesianum* 16 (1954): 386–422, 622–77. Ibid., 17 (1955): 120–55, 319–90, 611–53. Ibid., 18 (1956): 578–640.

Smith, M. *Clement of Alexandria and a Secret Gospel of Mark*. Cambridge, Mass., 1973.

Strack, H. L., and Billerbeck, P. *Kommentar zum Neuen Testament aus Talmud und Midrasch*, vols. 1–4. Munich, 1922–28.

Thurston, H. "The Holy Shroud as a Scientific Problem." *The Month* 101 (1903): 162–79.

"The Holy Shroud and the Verdict of History." *The Month* 101 (1903): 17–29.

Tobler, T., et al., eds. *Itinera Hierosolymitana et descriptiones Terrae Sanctae Bellis Sacris Anteriora et Latina Lingua Exarata*, vols. 1 and 2. Geneva, (1) 1879, (2) 1885.

Tzaferis, V. "Jewish Tombs at and near Giv'at ha-Mivtar, Jerusalem." *Israel Exploration Journal* 20 (1970): 18–32.

Vaccari, A. "Recenti publicazioni sulla santa sindone." *Salesianum* 15 (1953): 673–676.

Vignon, P. *The Shroud of Christ*. Translated from the French. Westminster, 1902.

*Le Saint Suaire de Turin devant la science, l'archéologie, l'histoire, l'iconographie, la logique*. Paris, 1938.

Von Dobschuetz, E. *Christusbilder: Texte und Untersuchungen zur geschichte der altchristlichen Literatur*, edited by Gebhardt and Harnack, New Series, vol. 3, pts. 1–4. Leipzig, 1899.

Walsh, John E. *The Shroud.* New York, 1963.

Willis, David. "Did He Die on the Cross?" *Ampleforth Journal* 74 (1969): 1–13.

Wuenschel, Edward A. "The Holy Shroud of Turin: Eloquent Record of the Passion." *American Ecclesiastical Review* 93 (1935): 441–72.

"The Holy Shroud. Present State of the Question." *American Ecclesiastical Review* 102 (1940): 465–86.

"The Holy Shroud of Turin and the Burial of Christ." *Catholic Biblical Quarterly* 7 (1945): 405–37.

"The Shroud of Turin and the Burial of Christ. Part II: John's Account of the Burial." *Catholic Biblical Quarterly* 8 (1946): 135–78.

"The Truth about the Holy Shroud." *American Ecclesiastical Review* 129 (1953): 3–19, 100–14, 170–87.

*Self-Portrait of Christ: The Holy Shroud of Turin.* Esopus, N.Y., 1954.

# About the Author

Thomas Humber is a free-lance writer and editor. Prior to writing *The Fifth Gospel,* he collaborated with psychoanalyst Dr. Robert U. Akeret on *Not By Words Alone* and *Photoanalysis* (the paperback edition of which will be issued by POCKET BOOKS early next year).

Mr. Humber attended Emory and New York universities, and before taking up writing full time was, successively, an editor of the Literary Guild; Managing Editor of *Atlanta* magazine; Managing Editor of *Scanlan's Monthly;* editor of the *Fortune* and *Sports Illustrated* book clubs; and Executive Editor of the Berkley Publishing Corporation.

Mr. Humber lives in New York City with his wife (a former book editor and author of *52 + 2 Menu Treasures*) and son.